Getting a Big Data Job For Dummies®

Published by: **John Wiley & Sons, Inc.,** 111 River Street, Hoboken, NJ 07030-5774, www.wiley.com

For general information on our other products and services, please contact our Customer Care Department within the U.S. at 877-762-2974, outside the U.S. at 317-572-3993, or fax 317-572-4002. For technical support, please visit www.wiley.com/techsupport.

Wiley publishes in a variety of print and electronic formats and by print-on-demand. Some material included with standard print versions of this book may not be included in e-books or in print-on-demand. If this book refers to media such as a CD or DVD that is not included in the version you purchased, you may download this material at http://booksupport.wiley.com. For more information about Wiley products, visit www.wiley.com.

Library of Congress Control Number: 2014935518

ISBN 978-1-118-90340-7 (pbk); ISBN 978-1-118-90383-4 (ebk); ISBN 978-1-118-90384-1 (ebk)

Manufactured in the United States of America

10 9 8 7 6 5 4 3 2 1

by Jason Williamson

Contents at a Glance

Table of Contents

• •

Introduction

The term *big data* was originally coined in 2008 by Haseeb Budhani, the chief product officer of Infineta, a wide area network (WAN) provider, to describe datasets that are so large that traditional relational database management systems (RDBMSs) couldn't handle the processing. *Getting a Big Data Job For Dummies* is for anyone looking to explore big data as a career field. In this book, you gain a prescriptive guide to finding a job — from planning your education and do-it-yourself training to preparing for interviews. This book isn't a technical manual on big data; instead, it's a playbook for starting your career in this emerging field.

If you want to go deep on big data, check out *Big Data For Dummies,* by Judith Hurwitz, Alan Nugent, Dr. Fern Halper, and Marcia Kaufman (Wiley).

About This Book

The world isn't short on books touting the benefits of big data, guides to using the technology, and white papers selling some big data solution. What has been missing is a clear guide to help people understand what it takes to actually become a big data practitioner. Delivered in the rich tradition of the *For Dummies* series, this book is a clear guide in how to chart your journey into the big data world.

You can use this book to find out how to manage your entrance into this new field, gain education you need, and stay current. Here's how this book can help you, no matter where you're coming from:

- ✔ **If you're a student or a recent graduate,** this book helps you understand the required education, tells you what it takes to land that first job, and offers a glimpse of what the future holds for you.

- ✔ **If you're a seasoned professional,** this book explains how to get the education you need to land a big data job. I walk you through whether to go back to school or start the do-it-yourself path.

- ✔ **If want to stay current on big data technologies,** this book gives you a jump-start on which technologies you need to know and how to stay current with the ever-changing landscape.

✔ **If you need to hire a big data professional,** this book shows you what to look for in your next round of interviews.

✔ **If you need help choosing a role or a company,** this book outlines the different types of roles you can fill within this industry and what kinds of companies or organizations use big data professionals.

Regardless of why you're reading this book, use it as a reference. You don't need to read the chapters in order from front cover to back and you aren't expected to remember anything — there won't be a test at the end.

Finally, sidebars (text in gray boxes) and material marked with the Technical Stuff icon are skippable. If you're in a time crunch and you just want the information you absolutely need, you can pass them by.

Within this book, you may note that some web addresses break across two lines of text. If you're reading this book in print and want to visit one of these web pages, simply key in the web address exactly as it's noted in the text, pretending as though the line break doesn't exist. If you're reading this as an e-book, you've got it easy — just click the web address to be taken directly to the web page.

Foolish Assumptions

I make a few assumptions about you, the reader. I assume the following:

✔ You have a basic understanding of the technology industry.

✔ You haven't been under a rock for the past few years and you've heard of big data and some big data concepts.

✔ You know how to use the Internet to find job listings.

✔ You aren't afraid to try new things. Big data is about discovery, iteration, and learning. You'll do a lot of that in this book!

Icons Used in This Book

Icons are the small attention-grabbing images in the margins throughout the book. Here's what each icon means:

The Tip icon points out anything that helps make your life a little easier. Work smarter, not harder.

The Remember icon marks information that's especially important to know. Instead of repeating myself (as I do with my kids), I use this icon. (Maybe I should make a little Remember sign to keep in my back pocket for my kids. Hmm. . . .)

 The Warning icon tells you to watch out! It marks important information that may save you headaches later on.

The Technical Stuff icon marks material that delves into a technical discussion of the topic at hand. You can skip anything marked with this icon if you just want the essentials.

Sprinkled throughout the book, you'll find stories about the job search process from people who are working in big data, told in their voices. Those stories are marked with the Anecdote icon.

Beyond the Book

In addition to the material in the print or e-book you're reading right now, this product also comes with some access-anywhere goodies on the web:

- ✔ **Cheat Sheet:** The Cheat Sheet offers tips on interviewing for a big data job and building your brand for big data. You can find it at `www.dummies.com/cheatsheet/gettingabigdatajob`.

- ✔ **Web extras:** I've assembled some great resources for you — everything from sample résumés and résumé templates to a skills assessment worksheet and articles on what to look for in a graduate school and more. You can find these extras at `www.dummies.com/extras/gettingabigdatajob`.

Where to Go from Here

If you're just getting into thinking about your big data journey, start with Chapter 1. If you have a few years in technology under your belt but you don't yet have any experience in big data, you may want to explore Chapter 4. To find out what life is like in various types of firms, check out Part III. Regardless of where you are in your process, you can find tons of information and advice throughout the book. Enjoy — and happy hunting!

Part I
Getting a Job in Big Data

For Dummies can help you get started with lots of subjects. Visit www.dummies.com to learn more and do more with *For Dummies*.

In this part . . .

- ✔ Understand the field of big data and why it's here to stay.
- ✔ Navigate through assessing your skills and interest.
- ✔ Get a handle on the big data players and the industry.
- ✔ Learn big data basics you need to know for setting out on your career.

Chapter 1

The Big Picture of Big Data Jobs

Some people have said that information is the new oil. There is a wealth of value locked up inside this new black gold. As with oil, the challenge is finding it, extracting it, and converting it to something useful. Information empowers new markets, innovations, and even transformation of societies. Like oil exploration, the challenge is discovering how to unlock potential value deep inside an ocean of data. That's the art and science of big data.

Big data has gone beyond the buzzword phase and into driving real value for organizations around the world. The Boston Consulting Group recently conducted a groundbreaking study that found a correlation between the use of big data and bottom-line revenue. It studied 167 companies in five sectors — financial services, technology, consumer goods, industrial goods, and other services — and found that those that worked with big data increased overall revenue for their firms by as much as 12 percent. Those are real dollars! The study concluded that leaders in innovation are more likely to credit big data as a significant contributor to their growth.

That's precisely why the market is seeing a significant uptick in demand for big data professionals. Firms are scrambling to hire knowledge workers who can help find new information wells of value locked up inside these vast fields of data. In this chapter, I explain why big data has arrived on the scene and what that means for career paths in this exciting new discipline.

How We Got Here and Where We're Headed

Why is big data such a big deal? You may be asking, "Didn't we *always* have lots of data with huge databases?" You may even be working on a DB2 mainframe database with data going back to the 1970s! Does that mean you're using big data? You may or may not be. When your datasets become so large that you have to start innovating around how to collect, store, organize, analyze, and share it, you're using big data.

Big data has come into the spotlight because of the convergence of two significant developments in recent years:

🖊 **There has been a substantial increase in variety, volume, velocity, and veracity of data.** We call that the four V's of big data. I add a fifth — value.

- **Volume:** How big the datasets are. Defining volume in terms of terabytes wouldn't be very helpful because datasets are growing every year. Consider high-definition video as an example: Each second of video requires 2,000 times more bytes than a single page of text. A 20-minute ultra-high-definition uncompressed video requires roughly 4 terabytes (TB) of storage. You get the picture.

- **Variety:** The different types of data formats included in your dataset. This is the attribute that comes to mind when people think about big data. Traditional data types (called *structured data*), including things like date, amount, and time, fit neatly in a *relational database* (a database where the information is arranged in columns so that they can be compared). But big data also includes *unstructured data* (data that doesn't have a predefined model or isn't organized in a predictable manner). It includes things like Twitter feeds, audio files, MRI images, web pages, and anything that can be captured and stored but doesn't have a *meta model* (a model that describes what the data is made up of) that neatly defines it.

- **Velocity:** The high rate at which data flows into an organization or system. Think of streaming video data from a security camera or tick data from a financial exchange. Velocity isn't a new idea. What makes it special in big data is the capability to sift through the information very quickly in near-real time. The trick is sifting the noise.

- **Veracity:** One of the key concerns of all managers is whether the data is accurate. Can they use it to make predictions? Inherent in all data are inaccuracies. Does this data have more inaccuracies than expected?

In addition to these four elements, I like to add a fifth V, value, which is the convergence of these four elements. Technology without value is just cool. What makes big data such an innovation is the fact that the intersection of these four V's generates tremendous value. It may not make the typical diagrams, but I certainly think it should.

✔ **The technical capability now exists to capture, store, and process this data into meaningful information** *quickly.* New data is being generated at a much higher rate today than in the past. For example, according to *MIT Technology Review,* in 2012 there were 2.8 zettabytes (ZB) of data but that number was projected to *double* by 2015. The advent of cloud technology, low-cost massive computing engines, and new innovations in data capture and analysis tools have made the capture and storage of this data a technically achievable goal.

Some examples of these datasets include

✔ **IT, application server logs:** IT infrastructure logs, metering, audit logs, change logs

✔ **Websites, mobile apps, ads:** Clickstream, user engagement

✔ **Sensor data and machine-generated data:** Weather, smart grids, wearables, cars

✔ **Social media, user content:** Messages, updates

As this field progresses, the amount of data, sensor points, and information will continue to trend up, as will our ability to mine this data for valuable and actionable information — information that gives managers the ability to make decisions about a business, product, or industry. What this means for you is that the job market will continue to see an increase in both demand and function for big data professionals.

Why companies care about big data

Companies care about big data because the promise of big data is transformational. The potential savings, new revenues, and innovations are limitless. For example, McKinsey & Company predicts that in healthcare alone, the application of big data has a potential value of $300 billion to the U.S. healthcare system, which is two times the annual healthcare spending in Spain. Organizations have realized that big data will increase their capability to compete by lowering costs or uncovering new revenue streams. Simply put, big data impacts the bottom line in a big way.

McKinsey & Company is a global management consulting firm with more than $7 billion in revenue and more than 13,000 employees. It serves as a key advisor to the world's leading companies and governments. Some of its influential publications include *McKinsey Quarterly* and research from the McKinsey Global Institute. Its 2010 research on big data became one of the major levers in driving global awareness to the potential of this new field.

The future of big data jobs

As an industry explodes, so do the job opportunities. The required functions of big data range from back-end systems administrators and model designers to front-end business analysis. The jobs can be for anyone from folks who are less technically inclined but have strong marketing skills to hard-core math wonks and everything in between. There is good evidence to suggest that many of the jobs will be located within the borders of one's own country. It is difficult to outsource big data jobs. One of the reasons for this is the fact that it is both difficult and expensive to move massive amounts of people around the globe. The requirement to be co-located near a business unit or field team is critical (see Chapter 4). A quick search on popular online job sites shows thousands of available big data jobs in the United States.

Exploring Big Data Career Paths

The types of roles in big data are many, but they do share some common attributes. And don't worry: They don't all require a PhD in math or statistics.

Not everyone is a data scientist

So, what is a data scientist? She is practitioner who helps the company achieve a competitive advantage through the use of the data. When the big data field began to emerge, people quickly jumped at labeling what they thought the corresponding job function would be. The term *data scientist* was thrown around in IT circles, but people weren't really sure what that job would look like. What emerged was the idea that big data can only be done by the most advanced mathematicians, statistical modelers, and specialized programmers. For many people, images of a Wall Street quantitative analyst comes to mind. (A *quantitative analyst,* or *quant,* is someone who uses models to determine when to buy and sell specific stocks.)

There continues to be a demand for traditional data scientists, but the field has expanded to include a broad spectrum of functions — in part because the advancement of technology has made using big data systems easier (see Chapter 7 for more on big data tools).

ANECDOTE

Thoughts from an experienced business analyst

I had an early interest in computing and technology when I was younger, but I really got started with data and analytics while pursuing an M.S. in management information systems at the University of Virginia (UVa). We had terrific professors, including Dave Smith, who taught a course on relational databases and database design. After UVa, I was fortunate to get a job as a consultant with American Management Systems (AMS), an early leader in data warehousing, where Bill Inman, who many consider the father of data warehousing, had worked. I worked on many business analytics and data-warehousing projects at AMS and spent time working with leading business-analytics software vendors in AMS's Center for Advanced Technology.

Over the course of my consulting career, most of my work has been in the digital space. One of my largest clients is a leader in the use of data and analytics in Financial Services, and I've learned a lot working with talented client and consulting teams there. My passion and interest continued to grow for the intersection of marketing and data, helping companies become more data-driven and leverage data to acquire and retain customers and improve customer experience.

One recommendation I have for folks getting started with data and analytics is to seek out and build relationships with others in the field. Connecting with others in networking groups, professional associations, and meet-ups, as well as through social media, is critical (and fun!). In the past few years, I've found blogging, Twitter, and LinkedIn to be particularly helping in making new connections and building relationships with others in the field. I've been able to use LinkedIn to build my brand through my profile and articles that I've written. When I write articles on analytics, I link to them in my profile (www.linkedin.com/in/dbirckhead), which allows me to continue to fully leverage my LinkedIn reach.

I think the exciting thing about big data and analytics is the rapid pace of change. In a recent study, the vast majority of marketers agreed with the statement that marketing has changed more in the past 2 years than in the past 50. Experience is helpful, but the pace of change means everyone has to stay humble, keep a beginner's mind, and make learning a daily and weekly pursuit.

—Dave Birckhead
Executive, Customer Intelligence Infinitive

Requirements of big data professionals

Big data jobs share some common requirements no matter what career path you choose. In Chapters 2 and 5, I give you tools to help guide you on your path, but if you're wondering if this career field is for you, take a look at the following list. Many jobs in this space require that people have experience with or interest in the following areas:

✔ **Marketing and analysis:** The process of using analytics to better understand the how's and why's of buyers in order to increase sales.

- ✔ **Product placement:** The process of getting products featured in movies and television to increase awareness and brand recognition.

- ✔ **Product management:** The process of creating products for commercial use.

- ✔ **Relational database management systems (RDMSs):** Foundational database skills.

- ✔ **Not Only SQL (NoSQL):** Methods for accessing data outside of traditional SQL programming.

- ✔ **Cloud computing:** Leveraging utility computing by renting for computer power and storage, paying only for what you need and scaling on demand.

- ✔ **MapReduce: A paradigm for dealing with massive amounts of servers in a Hadoop cluster.** Hadoop is a widely used programming model to sift through massive amounts of data using parallel processing.

- ✔ **Healthcare informatics:** Using data to drive innovations for healthcare.

- ✔ **Statistics:** Studying a collection or group of data for analysis.

- ✔ **Applied math:** Practical application of mathematics in the real world.

- ✔ **Business intelligence systems:** IT systems that allow business users to organize data into information to support business decisions.

- ✔ **Data visualization:** Software that takes information and presents it in a visual format for interpretation and analysis.

- ✔ **Data migration (extract transform and load [ET]):** Software tools to move data from one system to another and transform it into a structure that is usable by the target system.

If you're already knowledgeable in any of these areas or interested in these topics, you can feel confident that you'll be able to chart a career path in this emerging field.

Looking at Organizations That Hire Big Data Professionals

Most organizations today have begun to seriously consider building teams around big data instead of purely outsourcing this to consultants. Some industries are better poised than others to capitalize on big data. Some more challenging sectors — like government and education — will begin to accept big data as the overall data mindset as those institutions evolve. Overall, virtually every sector has a high potential for value from big data, but what that value means will depend on where you work and the mission of the organization.

Public sector and academia

When working in the public sector, the objectives are not to maximize profit for shareholders, but rather to create value for constituents. Public sector organizations work on everything from public health policy to defense. One use case for big data within government is in public safety. Imagine a world where border agents can make real-time decisions of the likelihood of a vehicle crossing the border containing illicit human traffic based on travel patterns of vehicles of known smugglers in ports of entry across the country intersected with image analysis, time of day, and crime activity in interior cities.

A *use case* is simply an example, real or hypothetical, that provides an example to illustrate a point or concept. The use cases I include in this book vary, but they focus more on how to set policy than on how to find profits.

Academia is similar to working for a public sector agency, but it often has elements of business because universities collaborate with outside companies. There is also a component of research and teaching within academia — the goals are advancing thought leadership in big data, as well as educating the next generation of big data professionals. For example, the University of Virginia's McIntire School of Commerce has the Center for Business Analytics, which is a partnership with leading companies like Amazon, Deloitte, Hilton, IBM, Kate Spade, and McKinsey to not only fund research in big data but also enable hands-on classroom experience for students at UVa to prepare them for big data jobs after graduation. Within academia, you find big data roles from research and education to business application.

See Chapter 11 for more on working within the public sector and academia.

Commercial organizations

Profits and value to shareholders drive commercial enterprises. The promise of big data seeks to drive net new revenues for enterprises across all sectors. Firms that are viewed as innovators are leveraging big data to drive real revenue to the bottom line.

The job market will only grow as more and more firms depend on big data for a significant portion of their revenue.

What parts of the business are using big data? The trend for using big data often starts within the marketing or product departments, with business units directly funding efforts, hiring consultants, and expanding the IT budgets. As the needs of the business grow, corporate IT — which is tasked with providing shared services across the company — are steadily adding these offerings to their services catalogues (see the next section).

You may find that in some organizations, *shadow IT groups* (those who have built data collection systems without getting explicit approval) are leading the charge. You will also find that some pharmaceutical companies are using big data for research purposes.

Corporate information technology

The function of corporate IT within medium and large companies is to provide computing services to the company. IT often maintains large data centers, outsourcing relationships, and software development teams, and creates IT standards for the company. Big data has been a particular challenge to traditional corporate IT because of the size of the data needed and computing power required to derive meaningful information from that data. However, life within corporate IT as a big data professional usually includes providing shared resources and programming capability for the business units across the firm. IT may be responsible for acquiring and installing hardware and software to run these massive data stores or leveraging the public cloud, which is a growing trend with companies around the world. More on these technologies in Chapter 3.

Marketing departments and business units

Marketing and business units own the profit and loss (P&L) responsibility for their product lines. They're charged with defining new pricing strategies, marketing plans, and products. It's no surprise that most big data projects start in these areas. Jobs in this group involve analysts, data scientists, and even programmers. Many corporate IT departments haven't gotten comfortable with or embraced the technology required to deliver big data. As a result, the business units often take the lead in getting this work done. They often engage with big data–focused firms and consulting companies to fill in the gaps that exist in their own groups. Some examples of these companies include Splunk (http://splunk.com), Tableau (https://www.guidancesoftware.com), and Jaspersoft (http://jaspersoft.com).

Big data firms

Many companies have been born out of the big data trend. They live to serve companies whose core competencies aren't in the big data space. Big data firms provide specialized software and analysis tools to enable companies to execute big data projects. Jobs in these types of firms involve creating and bringing new products to market that allow users to implement big data within their own firms.

Consulting companies

As with any specialized field, a consulting industry with experts emerges. All the major consulting firms around the world have embraced big data as a stand-alone consulting practice within their firm. Companies who cannot or do not want to fill internal roles will engage consultants to help drive best practices, train, and even serve as experts in residence.

Some of the global system integrators like IBM, SAP, and Oracle, which already have multibillion-dollar data analytics practices, are hiring specialists in big data to come up with new offerings and retool products for big data and the cloud.

Chapter 2

Seeing Yourself in a Big Data Job

In This Chapter

▶ Peeking inside the future of big data

▶ Building the case for job growth and the future

▶ Assessing your skills

▶ Moving forward pragmatically

I recently reconnected with a lifelong friend who had just climbed Mount Rainier in Washington. He said that it was the toughest physical challenge that he'd ever faced and that some of the people who have attempted to make the climb and failed were accomplished ultra-marathoners or Ironman Triathlon finishers. He told me that he had to train specifically to climb the mountain. It wasn't like prepping for a marathon or a triathlon. He had to take a focused approach to understanding the specific challenges to climbing and submit to the required training it would take to accomplish this feat. Even though there were runners who were able to run 100+ miles and were in better physical shape than my friend was, those people didn't have the specific endurance skills needed to climb a difficult mountain.

As you approach your professional journey, you need to identify the skills required to climb the big data mountain. This chapter builds the case for a career in big data and gives you a pragmatic approach so you can get to the top.

Planning Your Journey into a New Frontier

Think about your story and how you want it to play out during the course of your job search. You don't simply imagine your future job, and the universe delivers it to you. You need to make an intentional choice about your goals and then work backward to fill in the blanks with the story you want to be able to tell.

Consider where you are today. How did you get here? What life events impacted your situation? How did you react to things out of your control? How would you describe the past four years to someone you met at a party? Are there any parts you may feel you should skip? As you consider these questions, think about what you want your next four years to look like. Now is the time to create a great story.

Take a moment to be introspective about where you are today and tell your story. Andy Stanley, author of *Next Generation Leader,* says, "Experience alone doesn't make you better at anything. Evaluated experience is what enables you to improve your performance."

This is your chance to evaluate your past with the purpose of improving future performance. Don't get me wrong — I'm not implying that you are where you are because of poor choices. This may be a defining moment in your life, so take the time to evaluate where you've been.

As you go through this process, make it a habit to build in time to evaluate where you are so that you can avoid past mistakes and accomplish what you set out to do. You may very well have a great story to tell in a few years!

Imagine you've been employed for a number of years as a programmer. You've moved along in your company pretty well, learned some things, and had a great time doing it. Now, suddenly, you find yourself caught up in a layoff and the security you had was gone, the job market is scary, and you don't have clear view ahead of you. How will you react? What will your story be coming out of this time? One option is to spend some time thinking about your current situation. Assess your skills, set your sights on a new career in big data, make a plan, execute it, and reflect back on a challenging but rewarding period. That would be a great story to tell at a party in a couple of years!

Finding a Future Career in Big Data

Some people just seem to know the path they need to take because it feels right and they love it. Other people need a bit more evidence to validate their choice. As you look at the data — both empirical and anecdotal evidence — you can see that there's a fantastic growth opportunity in the field of big data. In this section, I build the case for the future of big data job growth and the overall global picture of the discipline.

The growth of big data jobs

A growing body of evidence suggests that the trend in demand for big data jobs will continue to grow, which is great news if you're just now thinking about your professional prospects! Not only are there thousands of postings on job boards and social media sites, but other evidence suggests that we're still in the very early stages of growth.

Both McKinsey and Gartner make huge claims about the number of big data jobs that will be available and unfilled in the coming years. In 2012, Gartner predicted that there will be more than 4.4 million big data jobs by 2015, and only about one-third of those jobs will be filled. McKinsey says that in 2014 the U.S. alone faces a shortfall of 140,000 to 190,000 people to fill big data jobs, with an additional shortage of 1.9 million analysts and managers. They say that by 2018, the U.S. won't be able to fill 50 percent to 60 percent of these roles. So, if you go with either conclusion, the job growth is significant, as are the opportunities for those who are prepared go after them.

Why is there such a gap? Three main factors that exist today suggest that demand for big data jobs will continue:

- ✔ **The lack of current widespread adoption of big data within organizations:** Combine that with the desire to take on big data projects in the future, and you have an opportunity for growth. A 2013 Gartner survey showed that 72 percent of respondents plan to increase their spending on big data in the coming year, but 60 percent said they didn't have the skill needed to do it. That's good news for you!

- ✔ **The amount of data being generated by customers, employees, and third parties:** Seventy-five percent of data warehouses can't scale to meet the new velocity demands of data entering the firm. In Chapter 3, I show you that *velocity* (the extremely high rate at which data is coming in) is a key attribute of big data. Plus, companies with more than 1,000 employees on average have more than 200TB of stored data. The 2013 Gartner survey results indicate that only 13 percent of companies are using predictive analytics today, so the gap between aspiration to deliver big data solutions and the capability to deliver big data is wide. This also means that it's ripe for opportunity for those who have the skills.

- ✔ **The amount of venture capital money being invested in big data:** Investors see the potential of big data and are already putting their money into these projects. Therefore, it follows that this is where the jobs will be. Position yourself to take advantage of these opportunities.

Predictions for the next several years

Predicting the future is very easy. Getting it right is the tough part. The question that many people have been asking is, "Is big data just a fad?" Now the question is, "How can I use big data today?"

Let's look at a few data points to support this movement away from big data being a science project to a reality. First, consider how search interest in big data compares to cloud computing over the past several years on Google. Figure 2-1 compares relative interest of searches on Google and compares the two topics.

The black line (the one toward the bottom) indicates the number of searches done in Google for "big data" during the period 2005 to August 2014. This includes searches for such terms as *big data analytics* and *big data PDF.* Google defines the number of searches as "interest" in a topic. The gray line (the one toward the top) indicates the searches done for "cloud computing" over the same period. This includes searches like *Google cloud* and *what is cloud.* You see from the figure that the interest in big data is now on an upward trend and the interest in cloud computing was very high and is leveling off but still has interest.

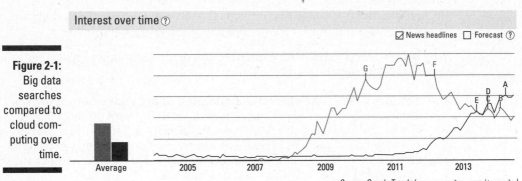

Figure 2-1: Big data searches compared to cloud computing over time.

Source: Google Trends (www.google.com/trends)

The top three IT areas of growth are big data, cloud computing, and mobile computing. Figure 2-1 shows that cloud computing is farther along the "hype" cycle than cloud computing, but both are key areas of interest.

It isn't a surprise that cloud computing had a high peak in 2011 and declined during the past couple years. People have a better sense of what cloud technology is. As a point of comparison, in 2013 Gartner pegged the global public cloud market sector at $131 billion, and says that it will grow to more than $600 billion by 2016. I don't think we can simply look at this graph and draw a direct correlation, but we can make a reasonable assumption that interest in learning about big data is a leading indicator for continued growth in this sector.

Here's what other analysts are saying about big data:

✔ In December 2013, the International Data Corp (IDC) a leading technology research firm, predicted that the market for big data would reach $16.1 billion by 2014 and grow six times faster than the overall IT market.

✔ Wikibon analyst Jeff Kelly's 2013 review pegged the big data market at $18.6 billion, with it reaching more than $50 billion by 2017. He breaks down market share between services, hardware/cloud, and software.

✔ SNS research predicts that the big data market will grow more than 17 percent compound annual growth rate (CAGR) during the next six years.

✔ Matt Turck's famous big data ecosystem chart tracked about 100 companies in 2010. His 2014 chart contains almost 1,000 big data firms.

Sizing Up Your Skills

Much of my earlier career was in modernizing aged computer systems. I was tasked with helping organizations take old systems and bring them into the future. We've all seen these systems — the ones with the green computer screens — at the bank, airport, or DMV. The fact is, these systems still run much of the core technology of major systems around the world. They're often 30+ years old with little or no documentation. We refer to the code behind these systems as *spaghetti code* because after years of adding new code on top of old, trying to trace a single thread of logic is like pulling out one piece of spaghetti from a huge plate without bothering any of the other pieces.

When I start on a modernization project, I always begin with a discovery phase, which involves doing a systematic analysis of existing code to document what the program does. "You can't modernize what you don't know" is my mantra. Once I know what the code does, I move to building the modernization plan.

The modernization plan includes some best practices for figuring out where you are today so that you can chart where you're going. Pay careful attention to doing an honest evaluation of these questions.

Make sure everyone involved in the project has the same understanding of what exists before getting started. If they don't, you may find that some are working at cross-purposes. This will sink the project.

Evaluating your aptitude for big data

You start by figuring out if you're a good fit for big data. The real question to answer is: What type of *role* do you want to pursue and how you are going to get there? Chapter 4 explores various roles within big data. Here is a short overview of those roles and some questions to ask yourself as you consider them:

- ✔ **Software developer:** This role is for programmers who largely support implementing big data solutions through software development. The jobs that fit these roles vary within an organization based on specific job functions. In traditional programming roles, developers are expected to focus on one, two, or maybe three languages in their day-to-day job. More often than not, it's just one job, like a C++ programmer or a Java programmer. Big data programmers are usually expected to be skilled in many languages and work at both the logic and data layers.

  Big data software developers have to be fluid and able to adapt to the fast pace of change. Can you shift gears between writing SQL, software logic, and back in three different languages in the same day, or do you like to be head down and focus on only a few tasks?

✔ **Business analyst:** Business analysts usually craft and answer questions to drive new insights, revenue, or costs savings for their organization. These people can be hired directly by the technology teams to help bridge the gap between the business owners and the technical developers.

Big data business analysts are expected to not only do deep traditional business analysis but also have technical understanding, as compared to their non–big data business analyst colleagues. Can you see problems from several angles? Are you able to get to the root cause of consumer behavior? Do you see the tie-in with information and business value? Can you build and execute a business model? Can you navigate between the technical and the business easily? Are you good in presentations to executives? Can you write well?

✔ **Data scientist:** This role tends to be highly mathematically and statistically oriented. Data scientists usually have advanced degrees and are involved with designing complicated modeling, advanced algorithms, and applied math. If advanced statistics, mathematics, and number theory are your thing, the role of data scientist is for you!

You should have a very high math aptitude if you want to be a data scientist. Do you already have, or are you working toward, a math or statistics degree? Have you dreamed of winning the Fields Medal since before you could talk? If you don't know what the Fields Medal is, you probably aren't meant for this job.

Figure 2-2 illustrates the four areas you need to consider in the following order: aptitude evaluation, skills self-assessment, plan to fill gaps, and execution plan. For example, when you have an understanding of your aptitude, you can begin to do a self-assessment so that you know what your education plan should be.

Doing a self-assessment plan

This part of the process may require you to conduct some research and additional reading if you aren't fully informed. It may take some time to write down the skills you have and the ones you need based on your review of job descriptions and discussions with people in your field. Rate yourself on a scale of 1 to 10, with 1 being "I've heard of it" to 10 being "I could write a book on the subject." A score of 5 means you're capable of executing that skill at a reasonably acceptable level in a professional setting — you won't be a rock star, but you'll get the job done.

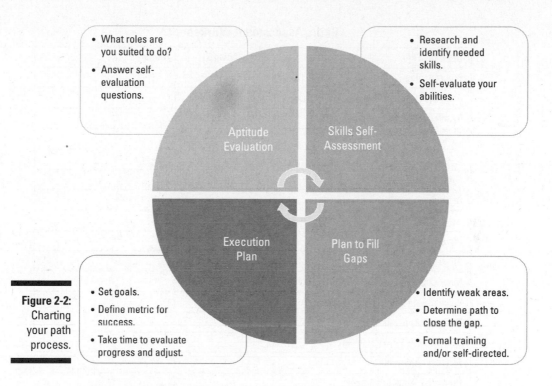

- What roles are you suited to do?
- Answer self-evaluation questions.

Aptitude Evaluation

- Research and identify needed skills.
- Self-evaluate your abilities.

Skills Self-Assessment

Execution Plan

Plan to Fill Gaps

Figure 2-2:
Charting your path process.

- Set goals.
- Define metric for success.
- Take time to evaluate progress and adjust.

- Identify weak areas.
- Determine path to close the gap.
- Formal training and/or self-directed.

As you glance at the worksheet in Figure 2-3, if you think you need some additional reading, you may find Chapter 4 helpful. Chapter 7 shows the various tools you're required to know for a specific role; this information can be helpful in filling out the following evaluation. *Note:* The list shown in Figure 2-3 is not comprehensive. However, a fair evaluation will give you a good idea about what you'll need to know and how you may go about building a plan for getting that job.

You need to understand your baseline numbers in relation to the amount of experience you have today. If you're a professional programmer with ten years of Java, you may enter 8 for Java and 3 to 5 on other programming skills. The key is to pick a value that you know represents your level of understanding. Then you can compare the other values in relation to that.

It's always a challenge to take subjective value and assign an objective number to it, but simply going through the exercise gives you a point of reference. It will be different for everyone. If you're a new grad or in the middle of college, your answers may only peak at 5 based on what you've been exposed to in school.

Skills Assessment Worksheet

Big Data Skill	Skills Rating	Notes
Programming		
Relational Database Design		
Relational Database Programming		
Java		
C++		
Python		
Hadoop		
Hive		
Pig/Pig Latin		
Spark		
MapReduce		
Visualization Tools (of any kind)		
Business Analysis		
SQL/Database Programming		
Financial Analysis		
Predictive Analytics Models		
What-if Analysis		
Business Writing		
Presentation Skills		
Mad Excel Skills		
Visualization Tools (of any kind)		
Data Science		
Statistics		
Math Theory		
Graph Theory		
Machine Learning		
AI (Artificial Intelligence)		
Signals Processing		
Natural Language Processing		
Visualization Tools (of any kind)		
Advanced Degree (Master's or higher)		

Figure 2-3:
Skill
assessment
worksheet.

Finding your gaps

At this point in the process, you need to identify what's required of you to gain a job. This depends on two critical factors:

- ✓ **Where you are in your professional career:** If you're in your early 20s and you're expecting a relatively junior role, you should work toward getting your numbers up to a 5+ (see the preceding section). If you're farther along and you want a leadership role or a senior developer role, the numbers have to be higher.

- ✓ **Your shortcomings:** Highlight those areas that are a 5 or below. Remember to think about this with respect to your relative potential strength given where you are today in your professional career. Those highlighted skills are what you need to work on to get that job.

Charting Your Path

After you complete your assessment, you need to figure out how you're going to learn what you need to know to get your abilities up to the level required to land that great position. Some of the skills you need can be accomplished through formal training, do-it-yourself learning, or a combination of both.

Chapter 6 tells you how to learn what you need on your own.

When to fill the gaps with education

Gaining necessary big data skills through formal education depends on several key factors:

- ✓ **Your best fit:** If you're focused on becoming a data scientist, you'll likely have to continue (or go back) to school for a master's degree or PhD. See Chapter 4 for more information.

- ✓ **Time:** Formal education takes time. The benefit is that you can easily track and predict when you'll be able to fill your gaps with knowledge.

- ✓ **Cost:** Training isn't free, and not all training is equal. Carefully consider the opportunity costs of *not* going to school and calculate the expected return on investment (ROI) if you do. Time is an additional cost you must consider. What would you have accomplished for profit or pleasure if you chose not to go? See Chapter 6 for more information.

✔ **Job requirements:** Many job postings require formal education and specific degrees as a prerequisite for applying. In highly sought-after jobs like top-tier consulting firms, the school you go to is also a contributing factor. For example, if you're going to work in the field of data science, you need a degree in statistics or math. If you want to work for a top-tier consulting firm like McKinsey & Company, Bain Capital, or Boston Consulting Group, you'll likely have to go to a nationally ranked top-ten school. See Chapter 5 for more information.

✔ **Desire:** Going to school or taking formal training takes commitment. It requires motivation over an extended period of time. If you're currently employed, this will be increasingly difficult — the demands of life, family, and work come into play. You have to be a self-starter and need a support system in place to enable you to finish strong.

The decision to change majors, go back to school, or pay for specific training is not an easy one. Because of the fast-paced changes in the field, rather than get a new degree you can probably get the training you need to land a job by taking vendor training. Objective and subjective factors come into play. Take time to think about each of these areas. The more data you have to reflect on, the better.

All this evaluation, recoding, and interpretation is a form of data analysis. Get in the habit of thinking in terms of inputs, outputs, and results. After all, you're trying to measure unstructured data here.

Filling gaps with experience

Many of the skills in the programming category can be accomplished through on-the-job training or self-directed education. This path is more easily accomplished if you're already employed with a few years in technology under your belt. The topics you need to consider are exactly the same as in the previous section with one caveat that lends itself to more self-directed study.

Emerging technologies that are pervasive are still relatively new and don't have a lot of formal training opportunities. The best way to learn them is often through hands-on projects or self-directed study. Conferences and trade shows and even the vendors often provide free hands-on boot camps with the objective to get people trained with enough skill to continue on their own. Check out Chapter 15 for a list of conferences and organizations that can provide these resources for you.

The best place to get more experience is from the job you have. Also leverage your skills. For example

✔ If you have ETL experience, this is directly related to the data component of big data.

✔ If you have user experience (UX) skills, you can easily translate them for big data projects.

✔ If you have database experience that can be translated into Hadoop or NoSQL. Oracle Exadata and AWS Redshift are relational databases to begin with.

Planning your milestones and timeline

The next step is to build a task list and write down your objectives as well as estimate the time it will take to get to the next level. This list will be based on your relative self-assessment. If you're already at a 5 for Python, for example, you may feel that to get to level 6 you need to execute a real-world project at work, or something at home or school that could be used on a résumé.

Figure 2-4 is an example of a list of tasks and associated times to learn those tasks.

Planning worksheet			
Item	Task	Duration	Notes
1	Learn Python	22	Currently at a 2; need to get to a 5
2	Hands on with Hadoop	10	1 to 3
3	Take on Hadoop pilot at work	22	3 to 5
4	Learn visualization tool	10	1 to 3 — Learning Tableau
5	Apply to pilot at work	22	3 to 5
	Re-assess	4	Re-assess skills and goals
	Total Duration	**90**	

Figure 2-4: A sample planning worksheet.

For the worksheet shown in Figure 2-4, notice that the tasks are building upon one another to construct a set of skills that can be translated into new projects at work or something that you can talk about on a job interview. I used 22 days to reflect the approximate working days in a month and 10 days for approximately two weeks.

As you look at this worksheet, you're asked to estimate the number of days it will take to complete the training. Figure out how to allot the time based on an eight-hour day. Is this a few hours a day at work, a couple of hours in the evening, or full time focus all day for 90 days? It doesn't really matter as long as you have a plan you are following and you understand how you will achieve it.

Fill out your worksheet so you can finish your project in a prescribed amount of days. Also notice that the last task is a task to evaluate what you've done (see the next section).

Measuring your results

When you hit your final milestone, don't forget to do the evaluation step. Many projects skip this step. Big mistake. Spend some time thinking about not only *what* you learned but *how* you learned. Was it effective? Did you accomplish your goals? What would you do differently? As project managers or team members, we have a tendency to skip this important step for several reasons:

- ✔ **We don't think we can spare the time to look back.** The reality is that you can't afford *not* to take the time. Otherwise you run the risk of making the same mistakes over and over. Reflections provide a framework to identify those errors and improve.

- ✔ **We think it's too expensive — time is money.** Lessons learned make you more efficient and profitable in the future.

- ✔ **We're afraid of being held accountable.** If we don't meet our goals, it isn't fun to sit around and talk about it. Rather than take a posture of blame, use the time to figure out how to avoid the same trouble again in the future.

The takeaway is to spend the time it takes to measure your results and reflect on the overall learning process. Let me take another moment to review the notion of telling your story. If you follow this process, you'll be able to demonstrate to future employers that your story is a really good one — built on careful planning, execution, and success with evaluation. Be intentional. Be reflective. Finish strong.

Chapter 3

Key Big Data Concepts

Big data has an extremely disruptive impact on most industries, and it's expected to change the way business leaders will plan and run their businesses. IT leaders are also challenged to manage their IT infrastructure and meet the new set of requirements driven by big data. IT vendors must redesign their products to meet the demand created by big data. Even though big data will impact most industries, the initial impact will be seen by selected industries that are more IT led and data driven than others.

In this chapter, I take a look at how big data affects several industries including risk and compliance, financial services, government, retail, and healthcare.

The Four V's of Big Data

The general consensus of the day is that there are specific attributes that define big data. In most big data circles, these are called the four V's: volume, variety, velocity, and veracity. (I like to add a fifth V, value.) I cover the four V's at a high level in Chapter 1, but I go into more detail on them here.

Volume

The main characteristic that makes data "big" is the sheer volume. It makes no sense to focus on minimum storage units because the total amount of information is growing exponentially every year. In 2010, Thomson Reuters estimated in its annual report that it believed the world was "awash with over 800 exabytes of data and growing." For that same year, EMC, a hardware company that makes data storage devices, thought it was closer to 900 exabytes and would grow by 50 percent every year. I don't believe anyone really knows how much new data is being generated, but we do know that the amount of information being collected is huge.

Variety

Variety is one the most interesting developments in technology as we digitize more and more information. Traditional data types (structured data) include things on a bank statement like date, amount, and time. These are things that fit neatly in a relational database (see Chapter 7). Structured data is augmented by unstructured data, which is where we put things like Twitter feeds, audio files, MRI images, web pages, web logs — anything that can be captured and stored but doesn't have a *meta model* (a set of rules to frame a concept or idea — it defines a class of information and how to express it) that neatly defines it.

Unstructured data is a fundamental concept in big data. The best way to understand unstructured data is by comparing it to structured data. Think of *structured data* as data that is well defined in a set of rules. For example, money will always be numbers and have at least two decimal points; names are expressed as text; and dates follow a specific pattern. With *unstructured data,* on the other hand, there are no rules. A picture, a voice recording, a tweet — they all can be different but express ideas and thoughts based on human understanding. One of the goals of big data is to use technology to take this unstructured data and make sense of it.

The definition of big data depends on whether the data can be ingested, processed, and examined in a time that meets a particular business's requirements. For one company or system, big data may be 50TB; for another, it may be 10PB.

Veracity

Veracity refers to the trustworthiness of the data. Can the manager rely on the fact that the data is representative? Every good manager knows that there are inherent discrepancies in all the data collected.

Velocity

Velocity is the frequency of incoming data that needs to be processed. Think about how many SMS messages, Facebook status updates, or credit card swipes are being sent on a particular telecom carrier every minute of every day, and you'll have a good appreciation of velocity. A streaming application like Amazon Web Services Kinesis is an example of an application that handles the velocity of data.

Value

I like to add a fifth V: value. It may seem painfully obvious to some, but a real objective is critical to this mashup of the four V's. Will the insights you gather from analysis create a new product line, a cross-sell opportunity, or a cost-cutting measure? Or will your data analysis lead to the discovery of a critical causal effect that results in a cure to a disease? The ultimate objective of any big data project should be to generate some sort of value for the company doing all the analysis. Otherwise, you're just performing some technological task for technology's sake.

Why is big data important to businesses?

A good example of big data usage is social media analytics, which enable companies to understand unsolicited public opinion about marketing initiatives, brands, products, and services in Twitter, Facebook, LinkedIn, Yelp, blogs, and other external sources where consumers post their opinions in public forums.

Social media analytics has become not only a leading enterprise business driver, but also a channel from which companies can get reliable feedback. Multichannel customer sentiment and experience has evolved to be a primary mechanism for understanding and influencing public opinion. Social media forces companies to be led by consumers. Industries that have stiff competition listen carefully to customers — and if they don't, they face loss of revenue or eventual death. Social media forces bad businesses out of business or into a better business service model. Companies are paying attention to the flow of information from external and internal sources. Although some industries are apparently deaf to consumers, it will change with the fullness of time.

Here are some of the marketing initiatives that chief marketing officers have begun to ask for:

✔ **Social media chatter:** Determine who is saying what about your brand and/or company. Brand sentiment analysis provides you with feedback you can't get from polls or surveys. What are consumers and the industry saying about your product?

✔ **Comparative analysis:** Compare your products, brands, or organizations to their competition. How do your company and products compare against your competition? What is the public saying in real time?

✔ **Marketing analytics:** Provide your customers with real-time information about the buzz or sentiment of your products.

✔ **Target marketing:** Dissect social media chatter about your subject from multiple sources in real-time and identify social media audiences for proactive marketing campaigns. For example, you may want to target your customers with special offers and new product launches.

✔ **Customer experience:** Mitigate issues and complaints before they go viral. Have you ever tweeted a bad experience at a restaurant or hotel and gotten a quick response from the company? I've recently done this about two experiences and was contacted by company owners within minutes. They did a great job of managing the customer experience by getting ahead of negative information on social media. Big data tools (see Chapter 7) can automatically process consumer feelings and prompt a response by companies.

Building a Big Data Platform

As we take the four V's to the next level, we have to look at how to operationalize this. Although volume, variety, velocity, and veracity are not inherently new concepts to the world, our ability to capture, organize, and analyze data is a relatively recent capability thanks to advancements in storage, computing, and analytics technologies.

There are generally four phases of building a big data platform:

- **Capturing data:** This phase gathers the data from the various sources and stores it into one logical location. Physically, the data may live within a data grid across different locations, but this step brings the information into one *logical data store* — information that looks like one big database to the user, or system, but is stored across a *data grid*, or multiple storage points.

Grid computing is combining the power of many computers to create a supercomputer. By slicing up jobs across a computing grid, you can achieve large amounts of processing power.

- **Organizing data:** Once the data is stored, it must be prepared for analysis. Organizing in this sense is the transformation and integration process. Here you have to take the data that is structured and the data that is unstructured and organize this in a data warehouse, relational database, and/or a next-generation file system and access store like Hadoop or NoSQL.

- **Analyzing data:** Now that the data has been captured and organized, it's time to apply analytics to discover what was once unknown but can now be revealed because of the available technology. Information is processed through analytics engines (see Chapter 7) and results can be presented to the users. Users run algorithms and apply visualization and execute queries.

- **Acting on data and measuring the results:** Here is where the value is realized. After you have results, the users can take action based on that data. The results of those actions can also be captured, organized, and analyzed. Analysis without decision has no value. This phase is the reason big data projects are started. Assess the analysis and make a decision.

Looking into Big Data Use Cases

Is big data strategy right for your organization? Well, all major corporations have big data, but they aren't sure what to do with it. All business leaders would love to have the actionable intelligence that big data can provide. For this, they must have a strategy. Understanding how big data can be applied to business is a key insight into getting a job in big data. The main reason why even most of the leading organizations don't have the strategy implemented is because they're slow to change. But this is changing quickly. The expectation that business leaders have today is high, and pressure on their performance is challenging.

Now, let's look at the impact of big data on a cross-industry basis: risk and compliance and supply chain, as well as four vertical industry segments: financial services and insurance, government, retail, and healthcare.

Big data in risk and compliance

One business area that has been vocal about the lack of big data storage, availability, and analytics is risk and compliance. Some industries, such as healthcare, government, and financial services and insurance, which are regulated more than other industries, may have more significant requirements for risk and compliance. They have to assess and make sure they're able to implement changes that conform to compliance guidelines.

Typical roles, departments, and groups within large organizations that need to access and analyze big data are

- **CEOs and CFOs:** They're ultimately responsible to the board and investors. Ensuring that all risks are covered is critical. Analytics from financial audits provide this surety.

- **Human resources:** HR maintains policy for corporate communication, performance tracking, and other human capital elements. Big data enables HR to make sure rules are followed and can provide tools to assist in research for conflict resolution through text analytics of email, for example.

- **Legal:** Often, legal must leverage emails, documents, and other work products as a part of discovery for litigation. Big data allows for supporting text research and archive retrieval of relevant information in various types of data sources.

Whether the need arises from litigation, external audits, and compliance investigation activities or from internal auditors, risk managers, and compliance officers, IT groups have the legal duty to preserve all relevant data, including electronically stored information (ESI) for litigation, audit, and compliance. This is easier said than done; ESI is a huge, disparate dataset, residing in many data sources that may reside in their own silos. Many of these systems don't interface or communicate well with each other. Everything relevant may include

- Transactional data
- Emails

 ✔ Documents, spreadsheets, and presentations

 ✔ Data on mobile devices

 ✔ Web data

 ✔ Multimedia files, such as audio and video and other multimedia files

For example, a company with 100,000 employees creates 100TB to 300TB of internal big data per year. One petabyte of raw data can equal 6 trillion records, which includes 185 million emails, files, and multimedia!

When a firm retrieves a notice of a lawsuit, or the reasonable possibility of litigation, two IT tasks are immediately triggered:

 ✔ A legal duty to preserve all relevant data, including all ESI (emails, IMs, SMS, faxes, documents, and transactional data). All relevant employees must be alerted to the danger of destroying data.

 ✔ An immediate need to quickly assess what the ESI says about potential liability.

Often, firms are not prepared to respond to the immediate requirements of modern litigation and electronic discovery because their repositories of ESI are scattered and/or not easily accessible.

An ideal approach would be a big data process service in place, which is a database solution that can be deployed immediately upon request. This service should be capable of ingesting several terabytes of emails, documents, multimedia, and transactions per day. After it's ingested into the big data platform, massive amounts of data should be searched at high speed, annotated, organized, and exported for production.

Ingesting data is simply the process of inputting data into a process or system.

IT's big data challenge

There is a significant growing demand for risk compliance and cross-analysis. Business leaders have begun to demand (from the IT vendors and their own IT organizations) cross-analytics of all data with high-speed results. Why is this a challenge?

 ✔ More than 50 percent of the cross-analytics tasks for legal, audit, fraud, and compliance data would be required to search tens of millions of database records. This would be a challenge for most IT departments.

 ✔ More than 50 percent of business intelligence, customer relationship management (CRM) systems, and enterprise resource planning (ERP) systems would be required to cross-analyze the structured data that resides in these systems against emails, documents, and other unstructured data. Current enterprise data warehouses (EDWs) — warehouses that systematized the retrieval of the company's entire data — don't do this well.

The result is that business users and legal and compliance analysts responsible for risk compliance require access to big data, but they simply can't get it in a timely and cost-effective manner.

From IT leaders' perspective, their primary objective is to reduce the burden on their IT organization and shorten or simplify their preparation process for the external audit, compliance, or investigation.

Business leaders' primary objectives are to

✔ Reduce the time (and related cost) external auditors spend on audits, risk compliance, and investigation of their company.

✔ Simplify and speed up the reconciliation process and provide more precise, detailed results (for example, loans or deposits downloaded to a general ledger).

✔ Reduce the overall burden of the audit on their IT department by providing the auditor selective, read-only, and self-service data access.

✔ Get early indicators of potential or existing fraud within the organization.

✔ Reduce preparation time, effort, and disruptions for the audit.

✔ Reduce time and cost of auditors (by allowing the auditor to self-serve her need for more data) and allow selective, read-only access.

Case study: Electronic discovery processes powered by a litigation response service

E-discovery is one of the early applications of big data. The primary consumer of e-discovery is typically the general counsel, chief compliance officer (CCO), and chief financial officer (CFO) of large companies. These systems are typically supported by IT (see Chapter 9). If an organization is presently, or likely to be, involved in any litigation (which is a possibility for any major company), it would be required to retain and produce the pertinent information when required.

IT would need, at a minimum, an email or document archive for the automatic and systematic retention of emails and other records. Most organizations rely on unstructured and structured data, yet most have the ESI stored in multiple repositories, such as email servers, backup tapes, shared drives, and relational databases, which don't interface well, if at all, with each other.

Every party to litigation is under a legal duty to preserve relevant data as soon as litigation is reasonably determined to be in the foreseeable future. When that obligation is triggered, a party must immediately take steps to prevent potentially relevant information from being destroyed. The litigation response team is expected to

- ✔ Preserve all relevant data by ingesting a copy of all enterprise data into a secure big data appliance. Some examples of these appliances include Teradata, Netezza, and Exadata.

- ✔ Cull the preserved data by using searches to identify the right dataset and reduce the amount of data that needs to be reviewed.

- ✔ Review and analyze the culled data by tagging this information for future recall. This is a way to index and organize information.

- ✔ Produce records to the opposing party, or export to another review tool.

One use case of electronic discovery involves a tagging process whereby records are categorized by type (email, documents, and transactions). Enterprise data can be searched using the search criteria required for the case. For instance, assume that a technology called Tesla is at issue in a patent infringement case; the user could do a search for all records containing the word *Tesla* and do a bulk or individual association of all matching records to a specific case number. Each email can then be reviewed in more detail to review for relevance, attorney-client privilege, or issues of special significance to the case.

Big data in financial services

Big data in financial services can have applications across many different departments and business units. However, I've seen some interesting applications of big data that are unique to this industry. Take insider trading, for example.

I was involved in a project being run by internal IT (see Chapter 9). This particular IT group supported internal security and audits. They were tasked with making sure employees within the firm weren't using insider information to illegally benefit on trades. Sometimes it can be difficult to spot insider trades if criminals are being clever.

Consider the following scenario: Say there is a nefarious person — we'll call him Snidely — on the inside telling a friend when to buy and sell stock. Worse yet, Snidely is also trading himself, but he's using his own personal device, like a cellphone, so he isn't on the corporate network. Snidely tells his friend, via email, when to buy or sell, but he uses code words to get the message across. In a firm with tens of thousands of employees, catching this kind of situation seems like a very tall order. Indeed, it is — but not for big data.

What this company did was use big data through text analytics and sentiment analysis to spot potential insider trading (see Chapter 7). There were several structured data items — like trade date, stocks, and amounts — as well as unstructured data — like emails and IP addresses of sources of trade data. The bank can quickly spot potentially fraudulent trades and send in humans to do additional investigation.

Big data in healthcare

Healthcare is another sector where big data is making significant impact, because of the following:

- **Regulations:** Big data analysis can provide policymakers with additional information for driving new guidance.

- **Patients' safety:** Big data can correlate drug interactions, patient history, and health to make a safer environment.

- **Quality control:** Big data can spot anomalies in drug production based on reaction reporting across the country and world.

The storage and retention of medical records, payments, and messages among patients, physicians, providers, and payers demand the need to have a big data strategy for payers, providers, device manufacturers, and pharmaceutical companies doing drug research. Cross-analysis of big data would also help tremendously with fraud, audit, profitability, litigation, and billing.

Case study: A medical college in Europe

A large institution for training physicians in southern Europe has 40 departments, 200 professorships, residency programs, internships, fellowships, programs for a degree of Doctor of Biomedical Sciences, and relationships with several large hospitals. To improve organization and the teaching process, the institution needed to drastically speed up generation and updating of documents for accreditation.

It needed big data to engage multiple sources for generating documents. The college was overwhelmed with a constant growth of documents, email communication, and database transactions that carry important information in emails, documents of all formats, and database transactions. Real-time storing, categorizing, retrieving, and analyzing within a unified repository were needed to have precious insight and power to eliminate the limitations the institute had.

The forensic medicine department needed to perform accurate, reliable, and fast conclusions and include vast sources of information such as reports, documents, audio and video records, emails, and data from multiple databases.

For overall and timely delivery of these conclusions, forensic medicine has a constant need to mix the big picture with a detailed view of the data in order to spot the right details and then decide what the next inquiry should be.

In most institutions, the chief commercial officer would play an important role in bringing a big data appliance into the organization.

Here are some of the key benefits that the institute enjoyed as a result of implementing a big data solution:

- It was able to implement real-time, recorded collaboration between professors, students, departments, and patients.

- It was able to achieve a 90 percent reduction in search time because of categorization of documents, emails, and database transaction stored in a unified repository.

- It was able to achieve a 76 percent reduction in purchase cost and maintenance cost.

- By implementing an active, automatic real-time email archive, professors and assistants were able to have full insight into email communication and related documents for particular teaching subjects or departments.

- It was able to promote fast, complex analysis of data using combined full text search and numeric analysis.

After the implementation, and to the college's surprise, it discovered new details and improved the overall view of its work with students and its scientific research. With the tremendous capabilities of big data, the college made big advances in two sections of its work: academic research and competent services delivered to the public.

The college is running a number of projects concerning the local society, but it also conducts health research that's important to the entire world. The big data appliance has improved the institute in several key ways:

- All project members have access to the unified repository and the categorized emails and documents needed for a specific project, according to their job roles.

- Alerts and notifications are sent out to the project members, immediately upon receipt of any document or email that has been associated with the project.

- The unified archive enables better and more thorough insight for the users and management.

The institute has been keeping pace with fast growth of data from its internal sources, approved external communications, and sources. In addition, the institute is taking full advantage of the full view and use of the information.

Case study: A major U.S. medical clinic

Answering questions from patients can be a complex task of pulling in general information and mashing that up with patient history. It can be challenging and time consuming to compile the best answers. This is a story of how big data enabled this.

The website of a major medical clinic in California contained all patients' medical test results. It had a "message center" that had all the patients' email correspondence with their staff (but not doctors so that confidentiality would not be compromised). Their "Ask Medical Advice" section allowed patients to ask questions to doctors and get answers from them. Patients could start e-visits with their doctors. There was an appointment section where the patients could schedule appointments and a prescriptions section where patients could review their medications and reorder them. Also a "My Health Record" section had everything about a patient's visits, inoculations, and so on.

There were sections for "My Personal Information" and "Customer Service," which allowed patients to see their billing statements, payments, and so on. "My Health Resources" had links for subjects, such as how to find a doctor, research health topics, and so on. This was a full-service portal — an all-in-one site. It contained virtually everything about a patient's health.

The clinic implemented a big data solution and put all this information on the big data server and gave access to its entire staff of doctors and nurses. Now, if a patient asks a question about problems with his prostate, all a doctor or nurse has to do is to enter the patient's name or Social Security number (SSN), and the word *prostate,* plus a time period, such as five years. The big data appliance then sends the staff all visits about the prostate, all prescriptions, all *STAT records* (records that contain the patients vital statistics) and reports, correspondence, renewals, emails the patient wrote asking about his prostate condition, medications, and so on. Everything is brought together with one simple request. With this system in place, a patient who might have a prostate crisis can call the emergency room, and the nurse will have everything there about the patient's prostate history in minutes. A doctor can study these and, if he wants, make a decision about the course of action even before he sees the patient.

Big data in government

Governments are the largest users of data. Federal and local governments have security requirements, sunshine laws that require them to have all public data available on the web, compliance requirements, and so on. Government agencies, regulatory compliance agencies, security agencies, and other agencies, need to collect enormous amounts of data, store it safely and quickly, analyze it, and provide actionable results to higher authorities. A big data approach can provide them with a data-centric organization (unstructured and structured) so that advanced analytics can be performed quicker and more efficiently with more precise results.

In Chapter 11, I talk about how big data could have prevented the Christmas Bomber board the plane. The following are some of case studies where government has successfully utilized big data solutions.

Case study: The U.S. Department of Defense

One of the departments within the U.S. Department of Defense, with more than 300,000 personnel, requested an advanced and independent system to monitor, intercept, store, and perform real-time analysis of all internal and external communications (email, SMS, MMS, Twitter, blogs, and file transfers) to detect any mention of restricted topics (for example, hazardous materials, confidential information about personnel, weapons, plans, installations, and other sensitive information).

Primary data sources were well defined, but the definition of *sensitive data* was not clearly defined and was expected to undergo constant changes. Plus, the type of search and analysis was also expected to change significantly over time.

One of key sources of definition of sensitive information are central systems that use relational databases as a backend and have frequent updates of sensitive information. The project goal was to develop, operate, and maintain an advanced system on a worldwide basis.

To significantly improve safety of air navigation and support increase in air traffic, the Department of Defense needed a solution capable of handling and leveraging increased data growth from disparate sources, including

- Emails
- Flight information
- Passenger information
- Data exchange services
- Telemetry
- Database records

Here are the key benefits that the agency enjoyed with the implementation of the big data strategy and solution:

- Allowed early detection of potential security problems by the instant cross-searching of emails, documents, flight information, database records, phone calls, and web clicks. Also allowed the agency to perform high-speed real-time cross-analysis.

- ✔ Reduced search time of new and historical data, therefore enabling immediate response for urgently needed data.

- ✔ Allowed real-time capture of emails, recording data to a CD, telemetry, and other data.

- ✔ Achieved a 91 percent reduction in cost of retention and deletion of emails, documents, and database records.

- ✔ Promoted collaboration with the Federal Aviation Administration (FAA), law enforcement agencies, financial institutions, and public health authorities to increase air transportation security.

The Department of Defense was challenged with real-time storing, classifying, retrieving, and analyzing of fast-growing data volumes from disparate sources, emails, documents, audio and video files, telemetry, and regular database transactions.

This big data approach also allowed government and law enforcement agencies to collaborate with the Department of Defense to further increase security. The Department of Defense was able improve transportation security, meet compliance requirements, and save money.

Case study: Law enforcement

When sophisticated cyber-attacks became frequent, and fraud and threats over the Internet reached critical levels, a European law enforcement agency didn't settle for a typical IP traffic monitor. Instead, it requested an advanced and independent system to intercept, store, and perform automatic real-time analysis of all communications (email, SMS, MMS, Twitter, blogs, Internet, and file transfers) coming in and out of the country and, internally, within the country. The purpose of the system was to provide data and analytic capabilities, with collaboration, to law enforcement agencies, health authorities, financial bodies, and transportation regulators.

The goal was to fight crime — specifically, to monitor security and health hazards, suspicious financial activities, and general threats. Without a clear definition of data or the type of search and analysis needed, the solution had to handle current and new data types, data sources, and forms of analysis. Two key requirements were

- ✔ Vendor support and the ability to update the system with new types of communication protocols and data formats.

- ✔ The capability to connect with banks, the Federal Bank, the Central Health Authority, and police by using standard databases and requiring the use of SQL in accordance with ACID rules (atomicity, consistency, isolation, durability) to ensure reliability. (See Chapter 7 for more on database operations.)

In effect, the law enforcement agency needed to develop a robust, enterprise-class big data solution with low maintenance and with the capability to connect to enterprise systems — quite unlike other programming-intensive big data solutions. Performance and scalability had to handle increasing data growth from disparate sources: emails, flight information, passenger information, biometric data, data exchange services, telemetry, and database records.

Here are some of the key benefits that this agency enjoyed as a result of the implementation of the big data platform:

- ✔ Instant insight into all inbound/outbound communications for the entire area because of the ability of a big data appliance to capture, process, load, and index emails, SMS, MMS, documents, flight information, database records, phone calls, web clicks, and so on. Now the agency could perform high-speed real-time cross-analysis at more than 20TB per day with data latency of less than two seconds. (*Latency* is the delay in moving data from one point on a network to another.)

- ✔ Cross-correlation of communication and cross-referencing with transactional data in less than 1 second for immediate response.

- ✔ More than 85 percent cost reduction of retention of emails, documents, and database records.

- ✔ Allowed controlled collaboration with governments of surrounding countries and health and financial institutions.

Case studies: A U.S. law enforcement and security agency

A U.S. law enforcement and security agency was challenged with real-time storage, classifying, retrieving, and analyzing of fast-growing data volumes from disparate sources, emails, documents, audio and video files, telemetry, and regular database transactions.

During the implementation of the big data solution, the agency received customizations necessary for this highly unique environment, particularly updates for handling of new data types and new protocols. Key benefits include the following:

- ✔ The law enforcement agency was able to improve security, meet compliance requirements, and reduce costs by 85 percent.

- ✔ Big data allowed instant search and cross-correlation of real-time data.

- ✔ The agency collaborated with other governments and financial and health authorities to increase security and effectiveness.

The system has since grown more than 300 percent compared to the initial installation, and handles data volumes as large as ingesting more than 20TB per day.

Case study: A European air traffic services agency

A European air traffic services agency needed to develop, operate, and maintain advanced air traffic monitoring for members of the European Air Traffic Space. Its primary tasks included technical maintenance, development, training, meteorological services, flight inspection, and calibration and Automatic Identification System (AIS)/flight procedure design.

To significantly improve the safety of air navigation and support an increase in air traffic, the agency needed a solution capable of handling and leveraging increased data growth from disparate sources: emails, flight information, passenger information, data exchange services, telemetry, and database records.

Big data provided the required analytical solution to the agency for the cross-correlation between unstructured and structured data. Some of the key benefits enjoyed by the agency included the following:

- Early detection of potential security problems by instant cross-search of emails, documents, flight information, database records, phone calls, and web clicks, as well as performing high-speed real-time cross-analysis.

- Reduced search time of new and historical data to less than two seconds, and enabled immediate response for urgently needed data.

- A 91 percent reduction in cost of retention and deletion of emails, documents, and database records.

- Collaboration between the government, the FAA, law enforcement agencies, financial institutions, and public health authorities to increase security of air transportation.

Big data in retail

Retail and e-commerce is another sector where big data has had a significant and disruptive effect. Every business transaction performed online can create

- A database transaction
- An invoice and a receipt
- Follow-up emails
- Follow-up voicemails
- Faxes containing order confirmation
- Records with shipping information and logistics
- Call center emails

✔ Emails about return and/or exchange of goods

✔ The need to reship data

No system today can easily present all the heterogonous information grouped together and searchable from the single screen. A typical solution for such a situation consists of an email archive, an email server, a database system, a data warehouse system, and a web portal.

Following are some of the business use cases where big data implementations provide retailers with significant advantages to improve their profitability while increasing revenue. They can build models that run against a big data appliance (unstructured and structured data) to achieve these objectives:

✔ **Making product and sale item decisions at multiple levels including store, region, state, and others:** This would allow them to forecast item and category movement based on the behavior of previous sales/events. They would be able to recommend the optimal mix of products to stock at store level and decide product mix for sales events.

✔ **Making pricing decisions and helping managers balance profit and unit volume:** The models would be able to guide decision making when balancing the need to move the most units possible with the need to make as much profit as possible. Price optimization models would be designed to calculate the perfect price to balance unit sales and profit. They would also be able to achieve optimum discounting optimization.

✔ **Assessing and managing co-movement behavior:** Analytical output would tell them which products will co-move during the normal business and sales event. They would be able to have the decision support at the store level. A store would be able to display items that co-move close together in the store or put items that co-move on a slight discount to drive more volume. With this type of information, retailers can also work with vendors whose products co-move to help sponsor events.

✔ **Managing cannibalization:** When the products go on sale, it's possible that customers will buy those products and substitute the sale product for another product they may have purchased. These models would forecast the results of putting items on sale on the volume of like non-sale items and the impact to overall profit. Retailers' decision-making process would improve and they would know which products they should consider putting on sale. They would have the tools to analyze the cost of cannibalization.

✔ **Helping retail companies acquire new customers:** This includes

• Behavioral segmentation to determine the actual customer demand segments

- Segment analysis for insight into buying behavior for specific customer groups

- Guidance to build targeted marketing campaigns for specific segments and the most appropriate way to deliver the messaging, including direct mail, email, print, TV, and Internet marketing for each segment

✔ **Deepening relationships with existing customers:** Acquiring customers is expensive and time consuming, but companies often don't have the tools to maintain and deepen their customer relationships. Customer behavior analysis would predict the next product purchase. Sophisticated loyalty programs augmented by models driven by big data would help build brand loyalty and deepen relationships.

✔ **Retaining customers:** Even with a store's best efforts, some customers will reduce their spending and select competitors' offerings. Models would be designed to anticipate these issues and proactively manage retention. Retailers would be able to anticipate customers who will be returning their products and/or not completing their contracts. Predictive models would help retailers understand which customers are most at risk of reducing or stopping their purchases.

✔ **Targeting for special offers:** Deciding the best offer to make to individual customers can be a challenge given the size and diversity of customers and their preferences. These models would be designed to help retailers identify customers' next likely purchases and calculate their propensity to make the purchases. They would also help identify the best customers to target with offers driven by manufacturers providing discounted pricing.

✔ **Making the most of marketing dollars:** When deciding how to allocate marketing dollars, these models would help marketing managers by removing the complexity caused by trying to understand the performance of historical campaigns in changing market conditions. Optimization programs would be designed to suggest the best possible mix of marketing programs based on user-driven criteria, including profit maximization and unit movement. These models would also provide flexibility to set minimum and maximum spend in categories and optimize the results. Simulation models would help predict outcomes driven by all categories of marketing spend.

✔ **Managing sales:** These solutions would also be able to help retail companies manage their sales associates. Managers would have accurate sales forecasting at employee, store, regional, and other levels that match the company's organizational structure. Multidimensional segmentation would allow companies to focus on key salespeople who have the propensity to improve or who are at risk for declines in performance. Salespeople would also have the tools to retain customer information and develop a personal relationship with their customers.

✔ **Managing inventory:** Managing inventory based on pattern recognition and using self-learning algorithms would allow companies to optimize their inventory and keep the lowest amount of working capital allocated to inventory possible while fulfilling customer demand. These tools would

- Automatically review the behavior of individual items and set appropriate order amounts.

- Use five dimensions to create a manageable group of inventory categories where purchasing rules can be applied. The typical dimensions are: item movement, variance in item movement, minimum order quantity, cost, and lead time. By segmenting in this way, the true nature of inventory movement can be managed and predicted.

- Create suggested inventory order quantities and manage vendor relationships.

✔ **Forecasting:** Big data implementations with forecasting models would bring tremendous value to the management of these companies, typically not available to most managers today. They would be able to

- Make forecasts predicted by the number of transactions that have occurred within a specific timeframe.

- Automate curve fitting.

- Be accurate at many levels of aggregation and require only a small amount of transactions to run.

- Quickly adjust to variance caused by external factors.

- Fix issues before they happen.

- Give eight to ten months of lead time on shipments.

- Integrate the forecast into annual planning, sales, marketing, and supply chain management.

- Shrink variance in ordering using additional data.

- Coordinate cash flow with the amount of product created.

- Reduce the ordering of unneeded inventory.

- Increase profits by anticipating and managing changes in demand.

Part II
Getting Your Big Data Education

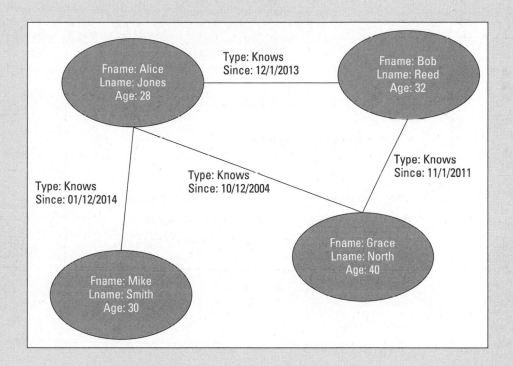

For more on what to look for in a graduate school, check out www.dummies.com/extras/gettingabigdatajob.

In this part . . .

✔ Find out what you need to learn to get a job.

✔ Understand the different roles within the field of big data.

✔ See how to create your do-it-yourself education plan.

✔ Discover the key tools and technologies needed to find a job.

Chapter 4

Roles in Big Data Revealed

They say that when someone is training to spot counterfeit currency, the would-be crime fighter examines the real thing with more intensity than the fraud. That's where examining real-world big data case studies comes in handy. In this chapter, I examine both the theory and the practical knowledge to help you craft your interview story and land that perfect job. I give you a look at different roles in big data along with real-life job posting case studies and interest assessments that help you gauge your interest in a particular big data field.

Big data is a tool. There are many dimensions to the roles available in big data. In this chapter, we'll build a foundation of different roles from a business and technical perspective.

Big Data Jobs for Business Analysts

Big data projects originate with solving problems with some business objective in mind. Much of the focus today centers around technology implementation, visualization tools, and data products, but it's important to remember that technology with no end in mind has little business value. Enter the role of the business analyst. Some people claim that this career is an endangered species, but there is some very good news for business analysts. Big data isn't just a new technology. It's changing the face of how we do business, and that means that the business analyst's role in big data is extremely important. It has been expanded to include that of business architect.

The basis for any of the roles discussed in this chapter often comes from the vision cast by business analysts. If you can envision a bridge that spans the gap between business and technology, you may find great success in this type of role. A business analyst can serve within a corporate IT division, a software firm specializing in big data, or a consulting firm. (See Chapters 8 and 10 for more information on life within these types of organizations.)

Some more good news, by the way: A recent Robert Half salary report shows the average salary for a business analyst is between $75,000 and $109,000, up more than 4 percent from 2013. Business intelligence analysts are seeing an even greater increase in starting salaries from 2013, with an increase of more than 7 percent. The market is demanding more analysts, and it's paying for it.

Besides the official title of business analyst, other possible job titles include marketing analyst, data analyst, and system analyst. (The term *data analyst* can also be confused with the data scientist's role, as I explore later in this chapter.)

Assessing your interest

In this section, I fill you in on some attributes you should consider as you evaluate your skills and interests. Spend some time reflecting on these areas. Do the skills self-assessment in Chapter 2. Talk to trusted advisors and get their perspective on you. Look back at your reviews from previous jobs or class reviews if you're still a student.

If you answer "yes" to many of the following questions, the business analyst role could be for you. Keep in mind, this is not an all-or-nothing guide. If you answer "no" or "not really" to a question, that doesn't mean you should rule out a role as a business analyst.

Are you naturally inquisitive?

The best approach to big data analytics is to come at business problems with the question/hypothesis perspective. Business analysts need the industry expertise (or ability to collaborate with industry experts) to identify the most relevant and most valuable questions to explore.

Can you see beyond the surface issues and go deeper into the problem? Do you know when a good idea has potential? Business analysts are skilled at sticking with a problem until they've found a solution. If you can drive hard and get to an answer, this could be great role for you.

Can you see through to the end quickly?

A friend of mine who is a lieutenant commander in the U.S. Navy often says he looks to develop an important trait in junior officers. He'll tell them, "Know the right answer when you hear it." In other words, do you know when you've uncovered the right area to focus on, and do you pivot quickly to focus your energies on solving that problem?

One of the biggest challenges in big data is that there is way too much data — not too little. Business analysts who can quickly see what is just a distraction and what needs focus are very effective.

Can you shift between creative and analytical?

I sometimes think of big data analysis in terms of an alternate blend of left-brain and right-brain activities. Creativity, curiosity, and imagination are all needed, as well as logic and rational and critical thinking. This is perhaps the rarest attribute. People tend to have a bias toward either creativity or logic, but the well-balanced analyst has the ability to see things at a abstract level and then to quickly go deep into the issue. Can you build a presentation for an executive to explain an idea and then write a four-page detailed document to explain the economics, technology, or implementation strategy? If so, you might make a successful business analyst.

Do you understand your audience?

One of the biggest opportunity areas I see right now is the improvement of how information is communicated to decision makers. Business analysts who can convert data into business opportunities and recommend action will rise to the top. There is absolutely no business value in data unless it translates to action.

Can you talk technology with the CTO and also explain the financial benefits of big data to the CFO? Can you help the marketing manager see the impact to her business unit? A good big data business analyst doesn't just understand big data technology and how it works; he also understands the impact to business and can speak the language of business.

Business analysts need to have people skills, as well as communication skills. They need to like to work collaboratively and make presentations on and off the white board. They also need to write, document, and negotiate.

Looking at a job posting

The job postings for business analysts vary based on the type of company — whether it's a consulting firm, a big data software firm, or an internal big data team for a corporation. These postings tend to be less specific in responsibilities and focus on solving business problems, good communication skills, and a balance of analytical ability and technology. You often see requirements for familiarity with Microsoft Excel, analytics tools, and database technologies. Largely though, the analytical skills are focused on problem-solving frameworks rather than database programming. A problem-solving framework follows a pattern for solving problems and executing on the solution. You need to be able to quickly identify the problem or need, find a solution, make recommendations, identify risks and how to avoid them, and describe what the action plan should be.

Consider the following job posting for an analyst with a big data focus. Carnegie Mellon University has published samples of business intelligence roles that recent employers have used. The following posting is for a business intelligence analyst, taken from Carnegie Mellon.

Business Intelligence Analyst

Each Business Intelligence Analyst is aligned with one or more groups, such as marketing, logistics, or customer service, and partners with those teams to help them achieve their goals. Whether you're measuring site performance, analyzing customer behavior and trends, data mining, or optimizing SQL queries, you'll be working with cutting-edge technology and multi-terabyte datasets. Working on the Business Intelligence team is a premier opportunity to develop a career in business and big data analytics.

At their core, Business Intelligence Analysts are strong in quantitative analysis. They enjoy coding but also want to balance that with their interest in business. They think critically to tackle complex challenges, thrive in a fast-paced environment, and are seeking a high-growth opportunity where they'll have an immediate impact on day one. Business Analysts are strong communicators who are eager to learn, are endlessly curious, take pride in hard work, and are committed to rapidly advancing their career.

Responsibilities include:

- Consulting with internal customers (for example, marketing, logistics, or customer service) to develop analyses that lead to actionable insights that accelerate profitable growth

- Wrangling data from multiple sources including sales, inventory, product, and customer databases to create integrated views that can be used to drive decision making

- Working with several large and complex SQL databases

- Designing and building reports and analyses in Microsoft Excel

Qualifications include:

- Highly analytical data junkie who enjoys coding but doesn't want to be a software engineer

- Positive, people-oriented, and has an energetic attitude

- Analytical, creative, and employs an innovative approach to solving problems

- Strong written and verbal communication skills

- Entrepreneurial spirit

- Degrees represented on current Business Analyst team include: Economics, Computer Science, Engineering, Physics, and Music

There are a few things worth calling out in this posting that can help you decide if this role is for you. In the list of responsibilities, the positing says, "Consulting with internal customers (for example, marketing, logistics, or customer service) to develop analyses that lead to actionable insights that accelerate profitable growth." What does that mean really? Analysts don't just have to understand information; they need to be able to articulate an action plan so that the business can capitalize on those insights. This is not merely a role that notices interesting things. This individual is expected to draw conclusions and drive action to revenue.

Case studies: Learning from the real thing

Examining real-world case studies from the marketplace is important for several reasons:

✔ **Looking at the real thing helps you hone your skills and target the kind of role you want.** The scenarios found in this chapter may not apply to the industry you're currently in, but they allow you to understand what may be possible in your industry.

✔ **It allows you to map your journey as you go.** If you can understand what roles your interests and skills fall into, the next step is to study the requirements of those functions and see how that plays out in the marketplace. By examining a potential narrative, you can create your own story.

You may notice that the specific company names aren't mentioned. That doesn't mean these case studies were pulled out of thin air. Often, when an organization wants to highlight its capability to deliver on a particular solution, the client isn't willing to disclose its name. It could be for competitive reasons. Rest assured that these case studies are based on real life, so you can believe them to be true even if the names have been changed (or removed in this case) to protect the innocent.

This role is technical, but you aren't expected to do heavy programming. Should you be able to code? Yes, but you probably won't be doing much of that. That's important for those who build those virtual bridges between business and technology — they need to be able to understand the components of big data solutions like appropriate technologies, software, or hardware needed to fulfill the business requirements. If the technology team has selected one programming language or model over another, the business analyst needs to be able to understand why that's a good or bad decision and how that could impact the overall outcome.

Finally, check out the kinds of majors that fall into this role — pretty much everything. Employers are looking for problem solvers who can find creative solutions and have the bias for action to drive real results.

Big Data Jobs for Data Scientists

Data scientists take the recommendations that the business analysts make and do a variety of tasks including the following:

- ✓ **Build the technical case.** They apply advanced math and statics to build the technical cases around the hypotheses that the business analysts build. Data scientists are tasked with building the models required to test these theories. This model is important to big data. You start with a hypothesis. For example, if we change the branding colors on a product on a given day and publish that on Twitter and it is positively received, we can expect an increase in sales of 4 percent. That is the hypothesis.

- ✓ **Create the mathematical models.** These models measure what positive sentiment means and then can model what tests need to be run to find correlations between that and price increases.

- ✓ **Discover patterns, trends, and correlations.** Some tasks may not necessarily start with a hypothesis. This is where the real power of big data comes in. You find patterns and trends you didn't even know existed.

The skill required here is to take a business idea and model it with numbers and data. Data scientists take that data and turn it into information. There can be a fine line between what data scientists do and what computer scientists do. There are some overlaps, but there are also jobs with a significant difference, namely in scientific and academic research.

Assessing your interest

As with the business analysts, there are a set of questions you can ask yourself to see if you're a fit for this type of job. Roles as a pure data scientist often require a master's degree or a PhD. So, you should carefully consider the following questions.

Are you naturally inquisitive?

Just as a business analyst needs to think in terms of building hypotheses, the data scientist needs to have aptitude in this area. Computer scientists need to be able to construct models that can prove or disprove a given business hypothesis. Can you see beyond the surface issues and go deep? Do you know when a result has potential and needs further testing? Are you passionate about technology?

Can you focus for a long time?

The journey required to complete a PhD or advanced degree in the big data field (see Chapter 5) can be a long one. You have to commit a significant amount of study to a specific area of research. Are there areas of math, statistics, or computer science that you have a passion for studying? Do you want to address big problems that may take years to solve? Do you like to write . . . a lot? Can you maintain intense focus on a few topics for many years — maybe for an entire career?

Are you self-motivated?

Data scientists need to be able to direct their own intellectual paths. Do you naturally follow a solution to its end? Do you have a knack for knowing where to find answers if you don't know them?

Are you multidisciplined?

Data scientists need to be knowledgeable in multiple areas — math, statistics, and computer science. Can you pick up computer science languages and concepts easily? Does the idea of a new language excite you or intimidate you? Can you easily collaborate with others to learn new things?

Idea to reality

Data modeling requires the ability to take business concepts and ideas and model those within a world driven by numbers and data concepts. Do you have the aptitude or interest to build experiments that capture the business value?

Looking at a job posting

Let's take a look at job posting for a data scientist who would operate at a junior level, or someone who has less than five years experience. The first posting is for an entry-level consultant, and the second would be more aligned with an academic or research-oriented position and was actually posted on several job search websites such as Indeed and SimplyHired. Both are grounded in math and statistics.

Data Consultant — Recent College Grad

Are you a recent college graduate who loves big data? Are you passionate about cutting-edge technologies and solving challenges for Fortune 500 clients? As a consultant, you'll be part of a team that develops and implements advanced algorithms and data pipelines that extract, classify, merge, and deliver new insights and business value out of structured and unstructured data sets. You'll work on a team whose data science efforts range from exploration and investigation to design and development of analytic systems. You'll have a chance to gain diverse experience across multiple technologies and create path-breaking solutions. You'll be surrounded and learn from the foremost Thought Leaders in the big data space.

This posting describes two paths: Data engineering and data science.

Key responsibilities include:

Data engineering

- Designing and developing code, scripts, and data pipelines that leverage structured and unstructured data integrated from multiple sources

- Software installation and configuration

- Participating in requirements and design workshops with our clients

- Developing project deliverable documentation

Data science

- Providing big data solutions for our clients, including analytical consulting, statistical modeling, and quantitative solutions

- Mentoring sophisticated organizations on large-scale data and analytics and working closely with client teams to deliver results

- Helping to translate business cases to clear research projects, be they exploratory or confirmatory, to help our clients utilize data to drive their businesses

- Collaborating and communicating across geographically distributed teams and with external clients

Required skills/experience include:

Data engineering

- BS or MS in Computer Science or equivalent work experience

- Experience programming in Java, Python, SQL, or C/C++

- Background that includes mathematics, statistics, machine learning, and data mining

- Experience with SQL, NoSQL, relational database design, and methods for efficiently retrieving data

- Prior work/research experience with unstructured data and data modeling

- Strong analytical skills and creative problem solver

- Excellent verbal and written communications skills

- Strong team player capable of working in a demanding startup environment

- Experience building complex and noninteractive systems (batch, distributed, and so on)

Data science

- BS or MS in Computer Science, Math, or equivalent work experience

- Coursework in mathematics, statistics, machine learning, and data mining

- Proficiency in R or other math packages (Matlab, SAS, and so on)

- Excellent programming skills in object-oriented languages

- Adept at learning and applying new technologies

- Excellent verbal and written communication skills

- Strong team player capable of working in a demanding startup environment

- Experience with Java and Python

Research Scientist Physiological Data Modeling

The Henry M. Jackson Foundation (HJF) is looking for junior and senior scientists to join the U.S. Army Medical Research and Materiel Command's Biotechnology High Performance Computing Software Applications Institute (BHSAI; www.bhsai.org). HJF provides scientific, technical, and programmatic support services to the BHSAI.

This opening is for dynamic scientists who are interested in

- Working with colleagues in other disciplines

- Applying computational solutions to biomedical problems

- Doing signal processing of time series physiological data

- Doing data mining, creating data-driven and physiological-based models, and working with artificial intelligence programs

The candidate should have a PhD in a related discipline and a strong publication record. The candidate is expected to simultaneously work on multiple projects, involving a diverse and interdisciplinary team of scientists across multiple laboratories.

Foreign nationals are welcome to apply. U.S. citizenship or permanent resident status is not required. This position is located in Frederick, Maryland.

The Henry M. Jackson Foundation for the Advancement of Military Medicine, Inc. (HJF) is a congressionally authorized, not-for-profit corporation that provides unparalleled scientific and management services to military medical research and education programs worldwide. Our mission is to advance military medical research. AA/EEO (Affirmative Action/ Equal Opportunity Employer).

Two main things are important to point out in these postings:

- ✔ **You don't have to have a PhD to be a data scientist.** The first role of a data engineer requires the candidate to have deep understanding of data modeling, programming, machine learning, and math. Although they aren't building complicated algorithms oriented around research like the second posting, this role requires a deep understanding of data and how to construct data to extract value.

- ✔ **There is some apparent crossover in function with the computer scientist's role.** The distinction is made around the matter of expertise the employee will have. The reference in the second role to having "a PhD in a related discipline and a strong publication record" means that the candidate has done real research in the area of big data and has published findings in an academic journal. This isn't just being able to spin up Hadoop clusters or create complex data stores. Data scientists have the skill and interest in using big data to conduct research and development. This requires a special set of skills and a desire and ability to publish in scientific and scholarly journals. The most significant aspects of the postings are having a foundation in math and statistics, data mining, and mathematical modeling. These are the everyday tools of the data scientist.

Big Data Jobs for Software Developers

Big data projects originate from solving problems with some business objective in mind. Much of the focus today centers around technology implementation, visualization tools, and data products. Today, businesses are doing more with less and need to show the return on investment in everything they do. Software developers are tasked with translating the business problems into workable solutions that drive revenue to the bottom line. (See Chapters 8 and Chapter 9 for more information the life of data practitioners.)

Assessing your interest

Big data jobs for software developers require many of the same core interests as other software developer jobs, but with a twist. Software jobs in this world are not static. Things change a lot — like new technologies, associated languages, software frameworks, and programming techniques. If you love solving problems with code, that's a good start.

Are you a team player?

This isn't just a cute cliché. The days of getting an assignment, going into an office for a few weeks, and coding in the dark are long gone. The industry is quickly migrating to the world of agile development, which focuses on software outcomes through a very iterative and collaborative approach. Teams are typically very small and co-located. You need to be able to work well with all stakeholders, not just your boss or team members, but customers as well.

Do you know more than one coding language?

Most software developers have more than one coding language under their belts. For a big data developer, that's just the start. Do you have the ability to learn and use new languages? Can you easily learn these languages on your own? Can you pivot between coding languages easily? In many big data software projects, developers need to be able to shift from using scripting languages like Python, to customizing a Hadoop job in Java, to turning a relational database data query. If you're more comfortable in predictable, steady-state software development, you may not thrive as a big data developer.

Are you ready to learn?

Not only do you learn new languages all the time, but you learn new techniques and frameworks. Big data is advancing so rapidly that staying current is challenging. The exciting thing about this technical advancement is that it isn't only around software — it's in hardware and cloud services as well.

A good indication of your ability to learn about big data is to look at your thirst for it. Are you constantly reading and trying new things?

Looking at sample job postings

The job postings in this section are for a big data developer and data scientist/software engineer. Notice that both jobs require more experience. You'll need to be able to demonstrate that the experience you have directly ties to the requirements. Think through all the duties you've had and see what skills have been developed as a result of that experience.

Big Data Developer

Support the creation of web-based decision support and analytic tools, using the latest JavaScript libraries. Maintain responsibility for the design, development, and sustainment of various existing and new web applications. Research and apply the latest web technologies to meet client requirements and develop rapid prototypes. Provide support to government and commercial clients, analyzing operational capabilities related to information technology functionality, integration, and interoperability issues. Perform research and analysis, support visualization design related to requirements traceability, portfolio management, and programmatic risk and health, and develop innovative scientific simulations and big data visualizations.

Qualifications include:

Basic qualifications:

- 5+ years of experience with object-oriented programming or entire software development life cycle in an academic or professional environment

- Experience with algorithm theory and data structures

- Ability to learn new programming languages and architectures quickly

- Ability to obtain a security clearance

- BS degree

Additional qualifications:

- Experience with researching, presenting, briefing, or communicating analytical material

- Experience with designing and implementing complex simulations

- Experience with rich Internet application frameworks, including AJAX, Silverlight, Flex, or ActionScript

- Experience with development of applications for scientific visualizations

- Experience in a rapid prototyping environment

- Excellent oral and written communication skills

- BS degree in Computer Science

Big Data Scientist/Software Engineer

You'll be working with a team of smart researchers and engineers to address challenging data problems in the exciting mobile advertising domain. The goal of the team is to make sense out of the huge amount of data flowing through our proprietary ad platform. The problems we work on include, but are not limited to, yield optimization, smart pricing, network behavior analysis and modeling, campaign performance optimization, inventory prediction, and management.

Responsibilities include:

- Development, research, and exploration in the areas of statistics, machine learning, experimental design, and operational research

- Propose, design, and analyze new algorithms to benefit our ad network

- Research and design experiments to evaluate different algorithms' impact on the network

- Implement and verify new algorithms, and integrate the algorithms into production

- Work with various other team members including data analysts, business owners, engineering, product management, and trafficking

Experience/skills include:

- Master's or PhD in engineering, data mining, statistics, operations research, math, physics, economics, or equivalent required.

- Two to five years of software engineering and scientific experience.

- Experienced with Java, Python, and big data.

- Experience with Hadoop, Hive, and Pig a plus.

- Prior ad network, big data, or analytics experience, operations research, or similar. Proficiency with databases, SQL, and scripting languages.

- Experience in data mining, data matching, machine learning, statistical techniques, experimental design, or optimization. Experience in extracting and manipulating extremely large datasets.

- Practical understanding of the mathematics behind modern machine learning, linear algebra, and statistics.

- Demonstrated ability to apply statistical techniques to solve real problems. Experience with data analysis, business intelligence, and statistical tools (for example, R, SAS, or SPSS). Analytical thinker.

- Ability to work independently and in a team to research innovative solutions to challenging business/technical problems.

- Attention to detail, data accuracy, and quality of output.

- Results oriented and deadline driven.

Saving half a million dollars with Hortonworks

Some organizations are skeptical about the value and effort required to implement big data solutions. You won't find the Clinical Informatics Group (CIG) at UC Irvine Health (UCIH) among them. They had a very clear goal when they looked at their big data storage issues. They wanted to make sure that when they moved their data to a big data solution, "no data would be left behind." They knew that Hadoop would allow them to store their files in their native format, so they migrated their data architecture on Hadoop onto the Hortonworks Data Platform (HDP). Not only was the project a big success, but they were able to shut down their legacy system. This saved them $500,000. Now nine million semistructured legacy records are searchable and retrievable in the Hadoop Distributed File System (HDFS).

Chapter 5

Foundations of a Big Data Education

*"W*hat do you want to be when you grow up?" My folks asked me that question well into my teen years. My usual answer: "I want to be a baseball player or a fireman — probably a fighter pilot." Well, by high school, I figured out that I wouldn't be getting any sports contracts, but I still wasn't quite sure. My parents would smile and encourage me to find a good "fallback" career, so I set my sights on computers and technology. Twenty-five years ago, we had majors like computer science, information systems, and computer engineering, but that was about it. Today the field of computer science and technology has grown in complexity, and a diverse set of majors has emerged to help people along the way.

The same can said of big data. However, it's such an integrated discipline — blending computer programming, mathematics, science (biology and chemistry) for bioinfomatics, databases, mobile, cloud computing, marketing, and business — that deciphering the right education can be a challenge. In this chapter, I explore different educational paths to a career in big data, whether you're just starting out or are a seasoned professional looking for a career change.

What's Your Major? Undergraduate Majors That Fill Big Data Jobs

Universities today recognize the growing demand for big data talent. They're building programs and classes around analytics, business intelligence, database management, and the supporting computer programming classes. There are two primary undergraduate paths to landing that first job in big data:

- You can find a major with a specific program in analytics and data science.
- You can tailor a traditional major with certain courses.

Tailoring your path simply means adding those classes or electives that you need to round out your skills so that you can compete for big data jobs. It's okay if your degree doesn't say "analytics" if you have a course load that fills the needs of potential employers.

The foundation of these majors can be found in one of three primary degree paths: math and statistics, computer science and engineering, or business. The one you pursue depends upon the type of role you want after graduation.

Math and statistics

In Chapter 4, we explore various roles in big data, including that of the data scientist. Many people pursuing the traditional title of data scientist (if I can call a role "traditional" in a field that's so young!) come from an educational background grounded in math and statistics.

Although you won't typically find specific degrees in big data, you will find specialized research programs and degree tracks that are useful to building your college résumé for data science jobs after school. Within math and statistics, you'll be required to have a deep foundation in probability theory, computational theory, and statistics.

These tracks tend to be cross-disciplinary in nature. This means that you often take courses outside the math department to build the required foundation for big data. You may find yourself taking programming classes from computer science and marketing classes from the business school.

In a recently funded initiative at the College of William & Mary, the department of mathematics received a grant from the National Science Foundation to build a program to help undergraduate students in the study and research of statistical theory and the analysis of very large datasets. Students who participate in this program finish with a degree in math and still are taking linear algebra, data analysis, probability, and statistics. What's different is that programs like the one at William & Mary bring the ideas of big data into the classroom. More and more labs, topics, and class modules put these ideas front and center.

Is a math degree from any university just as good as a math degree from any other university? Are they all equal? After all, 1 + 1 = 2 wherever you go to school. Here's the secret: Those universities that have invested real dollars in terms of both research and programs have a firm commitment to big data — not just in name only. Any topic of research that a professor is researching makes its way into the classroom. Has the university you're considering published any research on big data? What does the math department want to be known for in the academic world? Does the math department take part in joint programs across the university or with the private sector? If the department does, your chance of being exposed to big data topics during your educational experience greatly increases.

Computer science and engineering

Where the work of the classically trained mathematician is focused on modeling and number theory as it applies to large datasets, the software engineer/computer scientist is tasked with executing these models. You have to make it work in real life. So, a foundation in math and statistics is required for this field. Expect to be spending time in the math department. Don't worry — you don't have to go very deep into number theory and probability theory (you need cursory knowledge but you don't have to take a whole course in these subjects). You do need an in-depth knowledge (the kind that comes from taking a class in) of the following subjects:

- ✔ **Artificial intelligence (AI):** Artificial intelligence may conjure images of IBM's Watson on *Jeopardy!* AI is a field of study that tries to mimic human ways of learning in software. It's often used in text analytics and sentiment measurement.

- ✔ **Machine learning:** Machine learning is a subcategory of AI focused on developing computer algorithms that improves a computer's capability to process information through experience.

- ✔ **Data theory:** Data theory is the study of optimizing how to store, organize, and retrieve data.

This path allows you to explore technologies that make big data possible. You may learn the necessary skills to drive technical innovations in the big data field. For example, big data is key to cloud computing and provides the infrastructure needed to handle all that data. You may find yourself learning how to manipulate large data sets using software such as Hadoop. To learn more about Hadoop and how it's used in big data, turn to Chapter 7.

When people think about big data and the types of programmers who have been innovating in this field, a natural assumption is that progress has been pushed by database developers — the people who brought you common database technologies like relational databases. Technologies like MapReduce, NoSQL, and Hive don't come from database people; instead, software engineers created it because they needed a way to manipulate massive datasets that traditional relational databases systems couldn't provide. MapReduce is run on Google clusters every day.

Much of the practical wisdom covered in the math section earlier in this chapter applies to computer science and engineering. Does the computer science department or engineering school invest in, publish, or research topics in big data? Do the professors of the computer science classes express interests in the field? Do your homework. Check out their websites, surf faculty pages, and see what they're researching and publishing. If a school is invested in big data, you can be sure to get the exposure you need to prepare you for an engineering career in the field.

Many universities maintain their computer science degrees within the engineering school or the college of arts and sciences. In many cases, they reside in both. Furthermore, some schools offer both a bachelor of science and a bachelor of arts in the field of computer science, depending upon the school.

Business

A student once asked me what the difference is between a degree in computer science from an engineering department and a degree in management information systems from a business school. Much of the software engineering classes for both degrees are similar — both tend to require classes in systems design and database and software programming. My oversimplified explanation: In computer science, you learn how to make computers run fast; in management information systems or computer information systems or other technical business concentrations, you learn how to use computers to make money. Big data in the business school context is still technical in nature, but it's focused on solving problems in marketing, product placement, and buying patterns.

Building your own curriculum

If you're a business student with a deep interest in big data, but your university hasn't quite gotten its research and funding sights set on big data courses, don't be discouraged. You can build your own program by creating an interdisciplinary approach. Management information systems provide a solid foundation for big data. You just need to augment your coursework with some electives from the math and computer science departments, namely

✔ Probability and statistics

✔ Fundamentals of programming

✔ A class in the Hadoop framework if your university offers it

✔ A class in Java or a scripting language like Python

✔ A class in Ruby if available

After you've learned a programming language, you'll find that you can learn any language out there.

You can also take specialized online courses in specific areas if your university doesn't offer them. I cover online education options at the end of this chapter.

Business schools offer a wide variety of specific degrees in analytics with a rich set of classes in business intelligence, predictive analytics, and cloud computing. Although the coursework is not as technically demanding as the math and engineering paths, you'll be sure to get hands-on training in database design, analysis, and programming with statistics tools such as Hadoop and SAS.

As an example, consider the University of Virginia's McIntire School of Commerce. Students there can major in commerce and follow the typical concentrations like finance, accounting, and management. People interested in big data careers have the option of information technology and analytics, two separate concentrations. Business students at UVa have the opportunity to get hands-on training with analytics tools like Rapid Miner, training in programming Hadoop to do e-commerce basket analysis, and even training with cloud computing labs using Amazon Web Services. Although programs like this are unique, it's certainly a growing trend.

Continuing Education and Graduate School

You may not have known exactly what you wanted to do when you were an undergrad. You got a degree in something you were passionate about, but it may not have been all that marketable, so you chose to pursue a graduate degree. Maybe you have a passion for educational pursuits and research and you want to gain deep understanding in a field, so you find yourself considering a PhD. Perhaps you have your undergraduate degree completed, and you find yourself wanting to specialize in big data but you don't have the time (or energy) to go back to school full time. Yet you see the value in a formal, degreed education.

Education, like any other product, is demand driven. To that end, you can find a growing number of master's degrees in data and analytics and a growing number of people pursuing research in the same field.

Programs in analytics

Maybe you're an old dog that needs to learn some new tricks. That's okay. In fact, there are more programs in analytics geared toward working professionals than ever before. Every year universities are adding programs that sound something like master's in data analytics, master's in information systems management, or master's in data science. These programs are not hard to find and range in price from $30,000 to more than $60,000.

The format of these programs tends to follow the executive style or online only. Executive formats are for people who need to maintain their full-time day jobs; classes are offered at night or on the weekends. Similarly, online degrees can often happen in the evenings or at the student's own pace. In the executive format, the entire program can range from one to two years, with class time ranging from once a month to two times a month. A class is usually completed in an entire weekend, instead of over the course of a semester, like in a traditional format. Sometimes they require a residency for extended periods. With the market success of the executive MBA, the master's in data science is following suit. Top university brands are moving in this direction.

So, what does a master's in data analytics look like? In this section, I give you a look at a very typical plan. This one happens to be from Virginia Commonwealth University, but most schools follow something similar. This program is touted as a master of science in business with a concentration in decision analytics. The following is taken from the university's program material.

Prerequisites and foundation courses

These courses give you a sound foundation in business. You can come into this program without having an undergraduate degree in business. You have the chance to build upon basic business courses.

- **Calculus:** This is the first level of advanced math. It studies change.
- **Statistical elements of quantitative management:** This course uses statistics as a means of analysis and decision management.

- ✔ **Fundamentals of accounting:** This is a foundational course in financial accounting for business.

- ✔ **Management theory:** This class covers topics of organizational behavior and leadership concepts.

- ✔ **Financial concepts of management:** This course is about understanding key ideas for running global firms, including working capital management, capital budgeting, capital structure planning, and dividend policy.

- ✔ **Concepts and issues in marketing:** This foundational course is designed for graduate students with little or no undergraduate education in marketing. It's a study of the philosophy, environment, and practice of contemporary marketing.

Required courses

The following classes provide the basic skills and tools of the trade. They're both theory and hands-on oriented.

- ✔ **Business intelligence:** This class provides students with techniques and practices for modern decision-making in support of business/corporate performance.

- ✔ **Statistical analysis:** This class is an introduction to probability, descriptive statistics, and data analysis. It explores randomness, data representation, and modeling.

- ✔ **Management science:** This course gives students experience in the use of operations research techniques for solving organizational problems through the analyses of cases and management simulations.

- ✔ **Stochastic simulation:** In this course, students develop skills related to the application of probabilistic models in real-world situations.

Electives

Electives allow graduate students to explore specific areas that are of interest to them. They aren't typically required, and at least in this program, you only have to take two for graduation. Here are the electives this school offers:

- ✔ **Data mining:** Students learn how to extract complex information from datasets with modern-day data-mining tools and techniques.

- ✔ **Applied multivariable methods:** This class teaches statistical methods for answering complex business problems using methods like factor analysis and cluster analysis.

✔ **Forecasting methods:** Big data and predictive analytics require techniques to predict future patterns, behaviors, or outcomes. This class teaches common methods, as well as the tools to do this.

✔ **Quality management and Six Sigma:** Total quality management and Six Sigma strive to use a data-driven approach to gain efficiency and reduce errors in processes. This class covers the foundations of these subjects.

ANECDOTE

Construction engineer turned big data programmer

I came into big data midcareer, after spending many years as an engineer working for a construction firm. My path to big data took me through a total change in career — from being in the field at job sites as an engineer to going to graduate school.

For me, the move to big data and analytics wasn't due to a passion for the technology. Instead, I wanted to be in a field that I felt was growing, with large potential and cut across any industry. I haven't regretted the change. In fact, I've come to believe that a firm foundation in analytics not only makes for a great future for a programmer, but is critical for being an effective manager within any kind of business.

I went to the University of North Carolina-Charlotte to study mechanical engineering; after graduation, I attended Virginia Tech, where I earned a master's in mechanical engineering. From there, my career path in engineering took me to some great companies, and I eventually found myself as a project manager in the construction industry. That brought me to the late 2000s, and I had about 15 years of experience after grad school. The market took a big downturn and building and construction were hit very hard. Staying employed in my field required me to travel extensively for work. I was ready to start a family and didn't want to be on the road.

I spent time looking at what I could do, long term. I was searching for something I would enjoy and also keep me home. I did research on emerging technology, and big data analysis seemed to be growing field that could be applied to many different industries.

I knew I had the technical aptitude to do this job — after all, I was an engineer with two degrees. But I didn't have the skills I needed to do analysis. I had a friend who got into the field by going to graduate school, so I decided that was the path for me. I enrolled full time at North Carolina State University for two years and earned an M.S. in analytics.

Currently, I work at SAS as a developer for anti-fraud products as a programmer using analytics and data analysis to build products to identify financial fraud. Having a master's degree prepared me for the analysis and mathematics I need for this job.

Life at SAS as a programmer in analytics and big data has been extremely rewarding. My future is bright and challenging, and going back to grad school allowed me to be where I am today.

—Steve Uhorchak

PhD programs for big data

So, you want people to call you "doctor"? Then get ready to master a very specific set of topics. A friend once told me, "Getting a PhD doesn't mean that I'm that much smarter than other people. It just means I can focus on something the size of a gnat for a very long time." Well, of course he was a lot smarter than most people, but the point he was trying to make is that getting a PhD requires a lot of focus over a long period of time. That may sound boring if you're ready to go out there, find a job, make money, and change the world. But getting a PhD in math and statistics can allow you to do all those things, too.

Most hard-core data scientists, Wall Street mathematicians called "quants," and researchers in this field have PhDs in math or statistics. A PhD usually takes up to six years to complete. In the first half of your journey, you take foundational courses in how to conduct scholarly research, as well as advanced courses in your field. The latter part of the process is focused on writing a dissertation and defending that body of work to leaders in your field. Throughout the process, you spend much of your time writing, researching, and teaching. Lather, rinse, and repeat until you finish.

Pursuing a PhD is a rewarding path that allows great innovators to devote significant time and resources to advance their field of interest in a meaningful way. All of society, both public and private, reaps the benefits of these academic efforts.

Who you calling MOOC?

What happens when you take a community of the world's leading professors and students from around the world and open it up to unlimited participation accessible from anywhere on the Internet? You get a massive online open course (MOOC). Many MOOCs have the active participation from major universities around the world. The cost can be anywhere from very low to free, and depending on the program, recognized certifications are granted.

The following firms offer classes in specific areas of big data, statistics, and programming:

✔ **Coursera:** Coursera is a for-profit educational technology company founded by computer science professors Andrew Ng and Daphne Koller from Stanford University.

✔ **edX:** Governed by Harvard and MIT, edX is free, online, and open-source.

✔ **UDACITY:** Like Coursera, UDACITY is a for-profit system but it has content for vocational education as well.

✔ **MIT OpenCourseWare:** This is an effort by MIT to put all undergrad and graduate courses online and open to anyone. As of 2014, more than 2,100 courses were available.

If you're considering pursuing a master's degree in data science, either full time or in an executive format, and you're currently employed full time, taking a class is a great litmus test to see if you're ready for the academic rigors and time required to complete a degree.

Chapter 6

Making Your Own Way (For the Experienced Professional)

In This Chapter
▶ Finding the tools to learn
▶ Teaching yourself what you need to know

Maybe you've already been in the IT workforce for a while — and you have the scars to prove it. You feel the waters of change churning. You're thinking it may be time for a career change, and you hear big data calling your name. But you don't have the time or money for extra schooling. What you know is that big data is all around you, and you have the aptitude to perform well in a big data role. If this sounds familiar, this chapter is for you!

If you're going to chart your own path to a big data education, you should have an end goal in mind. Are you working today with business intelligence tools and want to become the next whiz in visualization analytics? Maybe you're a Java programmer and you want to retool your skills around Hadoop, R, and Cassandra so you can apply for a big data programmer job.

This chapter helps you think about how to identify the technical gaps you may have and build a plan to fill them. It isn't a cookbook, giving you the exact steps you should follow in order to magically become the perfect candidate for a big data job. That's because there isn't a specific set of steps that are guaranteed to get you where you want to go — you're building a career, not a soufflé.

Changing careers requires a certain amount of risk taking, self-motivation, and not being afraid of what you don't know. If you already have a background in programming, database management, or business intelligence, learning some new tools is a logical next step. If you have no background in software development, data, or math, your self-education may take more perseverance. But it's never too late to make a change, so if big data is your goal, stick with it!

School: It's not the only answer

Many people believe that having a degree is like taking a magic pill. I frequently hear people saying, "If I just had a master's in math, I could apply for that job." It's true that many recruiters use the academic pedigree to weed out bad candidates, but there are just as many stories of individuals who've gotten roles they wanted without checking every box on the job posting.

Is schooling important? Absolutely! Are there jobs you just won't get without a certain degree? Yep. Is it possible or even probable that you can get the job you want without that sheepskin? Yes.

So, should you go back to school? Well, that depends. If you have the time and money — plus the desire — to pursue a degree, why not? One key question to consider is: Will the payoff be worth the investment?

Most larger companies today will contribute thousands of dollars a year for their employees' outside education. If that piques your interest, ask your human resources department about the education benefits your company offers. You may be able to get thousands of dollars per year for continuing education.

If you're on your own for the cost of a degree, consider whether you can get the training you need some other way. In this chapter, I cover some great options for filling in the gaps in your education without having to enroll in a degree program.

Learning on Your Own Time

There are a host of resources — both formal and informal — that you can sink your teeth into if you want to educate yourself in preparation for a big data job. In this section, I cover the kinds of resources that are available, how you can access them, and what you can expect from them. (Appendix A offers some specific resources worth checking out.)

Hitting the books

The first place you should start is with a book. Many books can guide you from theory to hands-on examples. The benefit of a book is that it often can serve as a desktop reference after you've become comfortable with a topic. What you should begin with should really depend upon the type of role you're looking for and the level of exposure you've already had to technology.

For the business or marketing analyst

If your current background is as a business analyst or marketing analyst, you'll want to begin your research on some foundational topics like the high-level concepts of big data. Chapter 3 covers topics of the Four V's, but you can find entire books dedicated to volume, variety, veracity, and velocity. You'll also want to continue with books on big data use cases so that you can see how the application of big data applies to your industry. From there, you'll be able to understand common analytics tools, which you're likely familiar with. Chapter 7 and Appendix A cover many of these tools, which are used to tease out insights from structured and unstructured data.

For the programmer

If you're experienced in programming or database technologies, you'll want to read up on common modeling tools, languages, and scripting engines. Again, Chapter 7 and Appendix A give an overview of these resources. Make sure you understand common big data use cases, but from an implementation perspective rather than from a pure business standpoint.

For the database administrator

If you've been a database administrator, take the time to explore the new data models of unstructured data. Find out how to pragmatically model, access, and integrate the new data models with traditional relational database systems. If you haven't been involved in data warehouse projects, you should have a desk reference of those concepts. You'll have to bring together traditional relational database models, denormalized data warehouse concepts, and unstructured data all together to provide the backbone of a big data project.

Online tutorials

Some people learn by reading; others learn by doing. Online tutorials are extremely impactful — and plentiful — resources for getting started in a technology. There are two main mediums for online tutorials:

- **Step-by-step guides:** A step-by-step guide on the web carefully takes you through hands-on examples. It's very similar to working through a book, but it can be easier if you have large chunks of code to input and build. Just the other day, my son started out teaching himself Python by using a book. He spent a couple hours entering several hundred lines of code only to be frustrated with correcting syntax errors from his transcription. Although there is a lot of value in coding things by hand from the ground up, it can also slow you down, especially if you're already familiar with common coding constructs, logic, and data access methods. My son was happy — and frustrated — when he discovered that his book had some online resources and guided tutorials that would enable him to cut and paste his code into his editor.

- **Instructional videos:** Videos posted on YouTube or other video-sharing sites can provide a level of detail that some books and online guides cannot provide because you have the chance to actually see someone doing something in real time.

Online communities

The online community is extremely robust, especially for programmers and data analysts. Since the advent of the Internet, the culture of open collaboration has grown from a simple sharing of ideas to full-blown co-development. *Co-development* is more than just sharing ideas on how to solve problems — it's a community of people who work together to jointly develop software, usually under a collaborative, open-source license. Appendix A covers some of these open-source resources.

Online communities are great for people wanting to learn new technologies and concepts. Not only will you be able to get help on solving any problems you may have, but you'll be able to connect to others who have solved similar problems or are on the same journey. You can even use crowdsourcing to co-develop your ideas and allow it to become a full-blown project or even participate in one yourself.

Crowdsourcing (using the community of ideas to develop a great idea) is usually marshaled from an online community instead of employees of a company, but it can be used for commercial purposes. My Starbucks Idea (www. mystarbucksidea.com) is an open community designed to solicit great ideas from customers that Starbucks may turn into a product or service someday. Crowdsourcing has gained in popularity because of two main reasons:

✔ Companies found that utilizing outsourced talent who didn't necessarily expect financial compensation was cost-effective.

✔ Companies found that by allowing experts from around the world to solve problems, they could get better and more diverse solutions.

If you feel trapped in the tragic cycle of "How do I get experience if no one will give me a chance?", you can participate *today* by contributing code, ideas, or testing to a host of open-source big data projects.

This culture of open knowledge sharing is an amazing tool for advancing all technologies both for commercial and public or free use. Oracle is a great example of this. Oracle boasts to be the world's largest enterprise software company with the foundation of its massive revenue and profits being centered on the Oracle Database, not an open-source platform by any means. What many people don't know is that Oracle has been and continues to be a key contributor and tester for core Linux libraries and functions like Libstdc++ and CRFS. If the community can collaborate to move technology forward, both enterprise and the public benefit.

Can anyone test this code? The answer is yes. With open-source software, the source code is also submitted to the public, so any bugs or gaps can be tested by the public. The more eyes on it, the better it becomes.

There are several types of online communities to check out:

✔ **Boards and forums:** If you've been programming or using business intelligence tools for more than two years, you'll likely be familiar with the online forums, the most common and easiest-to-access communities. Forums are where people can post questions, code, and errors on specific topics, and the community of other readers can respond. Sometimes it's moderated by a leader, and sometimes solely by other readers. The conversation is archived so that future users can explore problems and solutions. When you start to query the Internet with your code errors or problems, you tend to migrate back to the communities that are most active and post helpful responses quickly.

✔ **Internet relay chat (IRC):** IRCs are simply chat servers that transmit text messages back and forth. Although IRC usage has declined during the past several years, there are still more than 500,000 active IRC channels. They're a great way to get connected with a community of users in real time. For Hadoop, the IRC channel is #hadoop hosted at `http://irc.freenode.net`.

✔ **Open-source development communities:** These are hosted communities on the Internet categorized by some sort of open-source project. Here someone — either a single individual or a group — posts source code for some software application, and then people contribute to all the coding and testing of that application. End-users of these applications are freely able to download the source code and can do with it what they want, within the confines of the open-source license. This is a wonderful way to get quickly plugged into a community as a project contributor or a tester. You may even want to offer up your own project to the community at some point.

Here are some open-source development communities worth checking out:

- **GitHub (`http://github.com`):** An online repository that facilitates collaboration among programmers. Projects can be both public and private.

- **Google Developers (`http://developers.google.com`):** An online repository for projects based on Google applications.

- **SourceForge (`http://sourceforge.net`):** An online repository for storing open and free software projects.

✔ **Software foundations:** Software foundations are usually formal nonprofit organizations that started as simple open-source projects that matured over time because of widespread adoption. Classic examples of these are the following:

- **PHP (`http://php.net`):** Home to the one of the predominate web programming languages.

- **The Apache Software Foundation (`http://apache.org`):** Hosts all the Apache open-source projects, including the Hadoop framework.
- **Python (`http://python.org`):** Python is a widely used scripting language with a wide level of adoption. Many big data projects are implemented using Python.

Membership is open to the public but is tightly controlled by the organizations. They still have the same characteristics as smaller open-source projects found on GitHub, for example, but with a greater degree of support, documentation, and active discussion.

On-the-job training

The best way to get a high-value education is to be proactive and find projects that you can learn where you work. For many people, finding their way into projects outside their specific area of expertise can be challenging in the workplace. Two factors affect your ability to find on-the-job training:

- ✔ **The climate of the workplace:** Does leadership encourage innovation? Are there avenues to submit new ideas? Can you take training — internal or external — to develop your skills?

- ✔ **You:** How willing are you to go outside your comfort zone to do what it takes to achieve your goals? Are you willing to put the required time in to learn new things? Are you willing to leverage your network colleagues and friends to get involved in new projects while maintaining your current workload?

You can't control the climate of your workplace, but you can control how proactive you are. And the good news is, you're more important than your workplace. If you have the right attitude and approach, you're sure to find opportunities — maybe in places where you didn't even know they existed.

Identify a project at work that you can volunteer for and perhaps get a new position because of it. Or perhaps you can develop something so great it gets you recognized within your company.

Building Your Own Big Data Test Lab

In this section, I explain how to build a pattern for some of the specific technologies, places to learn them, and a sandbox to practice. (A *sandbox* is a place to run a test.) It goes without saying that this section is *just* a sample pattern for learning core technologies and where to use them. You can start educating yourself in any area you've determined is a gap for you. The important thing is to find a project. There is nothing better than a goal to motivate you. So, pick a problem to solve. Figure out what gaps you have in technology and build a plan to fill the gaps.

The best way to learn is to do.

This use case is an example of how you can teach yourself big data skills by attacking a project with personal spending data. Suppose you want to do some big data analytics on your personal spending during the past three years to see if there are any predictive indicators or interesting insights you can learn by mashing up personal spending with the weather patterns in your city. Maybe you want to get a little more interesting and see if there are any correlations with your Facebook activity, status changes, or friends posting travel pictures. Who knows? That's the point: Try to find some interesting patterns. Right now, you don't know if any patterns exist.

You're trying to build some big data skills. At this point, you have enough knowledge of the required technologies needed to execute this project. What you don't have are the skills to make those technologies work. You'll learn these skills by doing.

The overall analytical goal is important only insofar as it gives you motivation and an objective. Success isn't based on whether you get any new insights; instead, you succeed when you've taken a step closer to learning the skills you need to land the job you want. If your goal is business analytics, tweak this project to focus on the analytics side and run analysis on an existing and publically available dataset. If you're trying to learn a particular programming language or data access tool, focus less on the business case and more on the tactical.

Although the following steps focus on learning new programming languages or analytics tools, this is only one pattern for learning, a best practice to help you build your own education plan. This example is not meant to be a tutorial in Python or Tableau. You can easily find more info on particular programs by using the resources mentioned earlier in the chapter.

To execute this project, you need to create a project notebook. It can be digital (using Evernote, OneNote, or Notepad), or you can just use good old-fashioned paper. Project notebooks serve two very important purposes:

- ✔ **They're pragmatic.** Notebooks are the place for you to document ideas, learning plans, technical notes, and results.

- ✔ **They're reviewable.** You'll find huge retrospective value (more on this later) in looking back at your progress.

Take time to journal your experiences — what's working, what's frustrating, and what you hope to accomplish while you're learning. Writing is thinking. Looking back on your writing is an invaluable tool for self-evaluation.

Step 1: Define your goals

Spend some time writing down your goals. Studies show that people who articulate their goals in writing are much more likely to accomplish them. *Be specific.* Here are some examples:

- ✔ Get comfortable with basic Python.

- ✔ Get hands-on experience with big data using social media data. Learn how to grab data from Facebook with Python.

- ✔ Learn a visualization tool (see Chapter 7) to combine personal spending with Facebook data.

- ✔ Complete this project within two weeks by working during the evenings and on weekends.

- ✔ Spend less than $100.

Step 2: Take a skills inventory

Spend some time defining what technology skills you need to accomplish the project. Using the goals from the preceding section (yours may be different), you'll be able to figure this out through your research on Python, reading forums, and just trying. If you don't know what you don't know, that's okay. You'll hit a bump and figure it out.

For this particular project, you'll need to know

- ✔ Basic Python.

- ✔ Database skills, such as MySQL and Excel as a data source.

- ✔ Tableau, a business intelligence and analytics software program.

- ✔ Facebook application programming interfaces (APIs), which are access points that allow two applications — the one you're building and Facebook — to communicate with each other.

Step 3: Mind the gap

Determine what you *don't* know and estimate how much effort it will take to fill in those gaps. Make some notes on where you think you should go for help. You don't need to look into a crystal ball and try to divine what you don't know. You're just estimating the work effort to learn things. You already know at this point that Python is a gap for you. Do your best to estimate how much effort you think it will be to learn it.

Step 4: Acquire knowledge

Start executing your basic learning plan and go make it happen. For this project, you'll start off getting basic Python skills. When you're comfortable with Python, you'll start making API calls to Facebook to understand how to access data and status changes. At this point, you may feel ready to do some more interesting work, like grabbing picture posts from specific dates that correlate with large credit card purchases you've made. You can build your skills along the way until you reach your goals.

Step 5: Look back

The retrospective step is extremely critical and perhaps the most important step in the whole process. The *retrospective* (borrowed from the Agile software development method, which is a process to do work in small iterative chunks) is a time to look back on the process. Simply put, a retrospective is the exercise of looking back at the endeavor for the purpose of improving future performance. You look not only at what went wrong, but also at what went right, because you want to repeat those successes again.

Do not skip this step. Just because you don't have a customer doesn't mean you don't need to do something this formal.

Begin to evaluate whether your endeavor was successful so that you can improve your performance. Here's where it gets fun! You're not looking for a binary answer — you don't just mark down a success or a failure and you're done. When teaching students about project success and failure, I tell them to evaluate project success through two lenses: process and outcome. You can evaluate whether your process was successful *and* whether your outcome was successful.

You're trying to get a job, so treat this retrospective part of the exercise the way you would any project you'd do for a client or your boss at work.

Process and outcome both have three levers, each of which impacts success. The three process levers are

- ✔ **Tools:** Were the tools of learning effective for you?
- ✔ **Time:** Did you accomplish this project in the time you expected?

✔ **Effort:** Was your level of effort to learn greater or lesser than what you anticipated? This isn't a measure of how hard something was to learn, but whether the difficulty met your expectations.

Here are some questions you can ask to illuminate this:

✔ Were you able to easily find resources?

✔ Where those resources easy for you to comprehend?

✔ Did you make the time to learn?

✔ Did you meet your time goals?

✔ Did you effectively use tutorials to learn new skills?

The three outcome levers are

✔ **Knowledge:** Do you now possess the knowledge you set out to learn?

✔ **Learning objectives:** Did you accomplish your learning goals? For example, did you get hands-on experience with Python?

✔ **Value:** Is what you learned relevant to finding a job?

Probing questions for outcome would include

✔ Did I learn the programming languages and software that I needed to (for example, Python)?

✔ Can I do this again with a different set of data with less effort?

✔ If I talked to my boss about this project, would she let me try something at work?

Look at each of the six levers of success and determine how successful you think you are. Doing this type of activity allows you to reflect on your process and outcome with the purpose of learning what went well and what can be improved. By breaking it down into the six levers of process and outcome, you can home in specifically on what to improve next time rather than just going on your gut. If you've been keeping good notes through the process, you'll be able to do this with relative consistency.

There are four possible states:

✔ **Success/Success:** Both process and outcome were successful.

✔ **Success/Failure:** The process was deemed successful, but the outcome was a failure.

> ✔ **Failure/Success:** The process was deemed a failure, but the outcome was successful.
>
> ✔ **Failure/Failure:** Both process and outcome were failures.

Here's a sample of a process/outcome evaluation. The more you write, the more you'll learn. I keep it simple here for the sake of illustration.

Process

Tools: Success. Effective use of online tutorials, forums, and videos. I learned a lot from texts and online tutorials. Whenever I had a question, they were answered by other programmers pretty quickly.

Time: Failure. It took four times as long as I thought it would to pull in Facebook data. I had to work past midnight every night, and I took a few multiday breaks.

Effort: Failure. Python was easy to learn, but getting Facebook status information into something I could use proved harder. Next time around will be easier now that I understand how to get around Facebook APIs. Tableau wasn't hard once I got it pointing to the right data. I still have a lot to learn, but I got the basic hang of it.

Overall: Process failure. Next time, I need to budget way more time to get this done.

Outcome

Value: Moderate success. I learned a lot about Python and how to mash up transactional data with Facebook status. I need to do a few more small projects before I would want to try this for real at work.

Knowledge: Success. I've developed a good working knowledge of Python and Facebook APIs.

Learning objective: Success. It took way longer than I thought it would, but I did learn what I set out to learn. I can use Python well and do what I need to do with Facebook.

Outcome: Outcome success.

Overall: Failure/Success.

Notes: I need to better judge how long things take for me to learn. Generally, I'm underestimating the time required. But I think if I did a similar project again, I could do it faster because I know where to go to get information. Also, I've improved my framework for learning and know where I tend to waste time.

Chapter 7

Knowing Your Big Data Tools

In This Chapter

▶ Identifying the tools you need to know

▶ Delving into data storage and access tools

▶ Staying current in the evolving big data world

This chapter gives you a high-level view of the technologies that companies use for building big data infrastructures. I cover the application of technologies like Hadoop, NoSQL, and visualization tools, as well as the role of traditional relational database management systems (RDBMSs). The ecosystem of big data tools is expanding fast. If I tried to list every category, type, and vendor, this chapter would be out of date as soon as the book goes to print. So, I cover the core technologies you need to know, and from there, you can build your skill sets as the field continues to grow.

Large data sets are common in biological or environmental research (human genome, anyone?), Internet search engine queries, financial markets, information-sensing technologies (for example, wireless and radio-frequency identification [RFID]), and data streams such as those used by aerial drones. As healthcare and health records move from analog to digital, expect manipulation of large datasets to become a challenge there as well.

Big data has exploded due in large part to machine-generated data and social media. In the past, data was created by data-entry people and end-users. There is only so much data a human can create at a company, but machines can create endless volumes of data. With everyone in the world creating data on social media, the data volumes have exploded.

Big data isn't just about volume; it's also about variety, veracity, and velocity (see Chapter 3). The speed at which data must be analyzed to make informed decisions has rapidly increased. The influx of different data formats coupled with the unstructured nature of these datasets has increased our potential for analytic capabilities. To that end, we need to employ tools in order to realize this potential.

Database Tools You Need to Know

When people think about big data tools, the first tools that come to mind are often technologies like Hadoop, MapReduce, and slick visualization tools. These tools are an essential part of the ecosystem, but they all rely on a foundation of traditional data stores. In this section, I show you these foundational technologies as well as the emerging technologies often associated with big data.

The big data field continues to expand. In 2010, there were about 100 companies making products supporting the big data space. By 2014, that number grew to almost 1,000.

Table 7-1 compares the different types of storage systems and how they fare in terms of *performance* (how fast work can get done), *scalability* (the capability for the system to grow), *flexibility* (the capability to store lots of different kinds of data formats), and complexity (how hard it is to implement). I cover each of these systems in greater detail in the following sections.

How big is big data?

Big data are datasets that have grown so large they are awkward to work with using traditional hands-on database management system (DBMS) tools. Current limits might be terabytes (TB), exabytes (EB), or zettabytes (ZB) of data, and here are the basic units of data measurement:

Unit	Size in Bytes	Real-World Comparison
Byte (B)	8 bits	A letter of the alphabet is 1 byte
Kilobyte (KB)	1,024 bytes	Half a typewritten page is about 1 kilobyte
Megabyte (MB)	1,024 kilobytes	500 pages
Gigabyte (GB)	1,024 megabytes	500,000 pages
Terabyte (TB)	1,024 gigabytes	1 million thick books
Petabyte (PB)	1,024 terabytes	180 Libraries of Congress*
Exabyte (EB)	1,024 petabytes	180,000 Libraries of Congress*
Zettabyte (ZB)	1,024 exabytes	180 million Libraries of Congress*
Yottabyte (YB)	1,024 zettabytes	180 billion Libraries of Congress*

* The Library of Congress holds about 28 million volumes.

Table 7-1	Data Storage Systems Characteristics			
Data Model	*Performance*	*Scalability*	*Flexibility*	*Complexity*
Relational database management system	Variable	Variable	Low	Moderate
Key-value-pair data store	High	High	High	None
Document-oriented database	High	Variable (high)	High	Low
Graph-oriented database	Variable	Variable	High	High
Column-oriented database	High	High	Moderate	Low

Relational databases and SQL

Relational database management systems (RDBMS) make up the foundation of any big data project.

RDBMS systems were originally used for OLTP systems before the advent of data warehousing.

Relational databases are systems that organize data into very logical tables, much like a Microsoft Excel spreadsheet. Systems are built around tables, columns, and unique keys to access that data stored in rows using a database access language called Structured Query Language (SQL). People use RDBMSs to store structured data. Figure 7-1 shows a simple example of a RDBMS set of tables to describe students, classes, and their grades.

To access these databases, programmers utilize SQL to construct a *query* to ask for information.

The following code is an example of SQL. This SQL statement, or query, calls out the required columns and tables linked by a unique ID to get a result of the two students who happened to have grades above a 90. The key here is that unique ID, which is used to identify discrete rows within the database system.

```
Select student.first, student.last from student where grade.grade > 90 and
              student.id=grade.id

Result:
Mark Brown
John Good
```

Student

ID	First	Last
S103	John	Smith
S104	Mary	Jones
S105	Jane	Doe
S106	Mark	Brown
S107	John	Good

Grade

ID	Code	Grade
S103	DBS	88
S103	PM	90
S104	PR1	55
S104	PM	89
S106	PR2	94
S107	PR1	98
S107	PR2	84
S107	PM	83

Course

Code	Title
DBS	Database Systems
PR1	Programming 1
PR2	Programming 2
PM	Project Mgmt

Figure 7-1:
An example
of a set of
relational
tables.

This example illustrates two important points about database systems:

- ✔ **Storage:** Data must be collected and stored in a defined, or structured format (refer to Figure 7-1).

- ✔ **Access:** You must have a programmatic method to access that data. That is done through SQL. SQL is *not* a database management system; it's a standard language for access data.

This *extremely* simple example is the framework for how most of the world's data is stored and accessed. Even if you don't plan on becoming a database programmer, a good grasp of SQL will be required for any big data work.

A few key vendors today store most of the world's data. IBM Db2, Oracle, and Microsoft's SQL Server hold almost 90 percent of commercially available database management systems. Open-source products include MySQL, which is curated by Oracle and PostgreSQL.

NoSQL

A vast amount of information is stored on RDBMSs, but what about all the other technology you hear about? The huge amount of data and the need to access it quickly, as well as store unstructured data, requires an array of other systems that enable speed and agility. The advent of Not Only SQL

(NoSQL) — not to be read as a negative comment on SQL but in addition to SQL — provided users with a more flexible and scalable way to store and access data to accommodate the demands of big data. Often, NoSQL systems lack the ACID transactions supported by traditional systems. ACID stands for automaticity, consistency, isolation, and durability; it refers to a set of attributes that ensures *transaction integrity* (the correct recording of a transaction) in a database — for example, a bank withdrawal is correctly recorded. The following sections discuss common NoSQL technologies.

Key-value-pair data stores

This system does not require a highly structured model like a relational system. The key-value-pair (KVP) system focuses on tables and keys, allows for great flexibility, and can grow to a very large sizes without sacrificing performance. This is called *scale. Scaling,* or adding millions or billions of items to a data store, can impact performance negatively in a traditional system. KVP stores that "scale well" can get very, very big and still perform fast.

A *key* is a identifier that is used to find a *value,* the thing you want to store. Together they're considered a *pair.*

Figure 7-2 shows how these tables work. Say you want to store user preferences like favorite fruit, car, color, and sport. To access that information, you would simply query the key, which could have been retrieved from a *browser cookie* (a piece of code put in the user's browser by a company to determine what the user does when he visits the user's site) and retrieve that data. The "system" in this case allows you to programmatically store and query the key-value-pair. Querying a key simply means looking it up and getting the value. The KVP system offers enormous flexibility for a situation like this where you don't want to restrict storage choices. When you need to store billions of items of data, a traditional RDMS can perform poorly.

The hard part is trying to make sense of that table on the right in Figure 7-2. Let's take the browser cookie example a little further. Say you manage a very popular website and need to track where users are coming from. Do they originate from Google, Yahoo!, or somewhere else? You would be able to store an IP address of a user as a key and the value could be the originating web page. This table could contain a snapshot of millions of users, and combing through that information could be a challenge.

Preferences

Key	Value
Fruit	Apple
Car	Volvo
Color	Green
Sport	Basketball

Preferences

Key	Value
Fbuse123_Fruit	Apple
LinkIn342_Car	Volvo
Twtr122_Color	Pink
Tumbl323_Sport	Golf

Figure 7-2:
The key-value pair model.

KVP solutions for big data are designed to be highly scalable and resilient. These technologies are typically stored entirely in random access memory (RAM), so access is fast and doesn't require the query to access data stored on a physical device like a disc drive, which takes much longer to access. These systems also utilize grid computing and parallel processing, which spreads simultaneous jobs across many computers to share the workload while ensuring fault tolerance if one section of a grid happens to fail.

Grid computing is a concept of spreading jobs across many computers to get the jobs done faster, as well as provide a high level of availability or fault tolerance. *Fault tolerance* is making sure a system can still run if something breaks. If you have many computers, or nodes, working together, and one fails, the entire job can still continue.

Prevalent KVP implementations include the following:

- **Amazon DynomoDB (`http://aws.amazon.com/dynamodb`):** A KVP NoSQL data store offered as a cloud service from Amazon.

- **FoundationDB (`https://foundationdb.com`):** A KVP NoSQL data store that ensures ACID transactions.

- **MemcacheDB (`http://memcachedb.org`):** A distributed (grid based) data store that resided in RAM.

- **Redis (`http://redis.io`):** A key-value cache with the capability to store all types of data — structured and unstructured. In the industry people refer to Redis as a data structure server.

- **Riak (`http://basho.com/riak`):** An open-source NoSQL KVP based on concepts from the Amazon DynomoDB product.

Refer to Table 7-1, earlier in this chapter, for how the KVP system compares with the other systems discussed in this section.

Document-oriented databases

Document-oriented databases allow for the storage and retrieval of *semistructured data* — data that's somewhere between unstructured (like a tweet) and structured (like you would see on a bank statement). Web pages and documents are a great example of semistructured data.

Whereas the RDBMSs are oriented around tables and keys, the document-oriented systems use a document paradigm. Instead of storing data in rows and columns, the document model defines information in a document and stores that information logically. This is a very flexible and simplified approach to data storage and retrieval. These model definitions are created by the programmer and accessed through the programming system. Plus, as with big data, users can more readily support real-time information capture, updates, and analysis that is more difficult in a tightly structured relational system.

Many of these NoSQL document databases store data in JSON format.

For example, in a case study published by MongoDB (a document-oriented database company), Intuit (a software company) needed to analyze website data from thousands of websites that Intuit hosted for its customers. With that analysis, Intuit would then make recommendations and improvements and help customers with lead generation and more access for potential customers. Traditional databases like MySQL and Oracle couldn't easily handle the variety of data that needed to be stored, and querying the data took a very long time. The document-centric nature of MongoDB allowed Intuit to take ten years of customer data and derive insights quickly without increasing complexity. These insights allowed Intuit's website clients to better sell to their own customers.

Popular document-oriented implementations include the following:

- **Cassandra (`http://cassandra.apache.org`):** A part of the Apache open-source project, this is a distributed (grid-based) document-oriented database system.

- **CouchDB (`http://couchdb.apache.org`):** An open-source document-oriented database system that has ACID capabilities.

- **MarkLogic (`www.marklogic.com`):** A commercially available document-oriented database system touted as enterprise ready. This is highly secure, reliable, and used by many Fortune 1,000 companies for customer-facing processes.

- **MongoDB (`www.mongodb.org`):** Perhaps the leading NoSQL database system that uses a document-oriented approach. This is also open-source under the Apache license model.

Refer to Table 7-1, earlier in this chapter, to see how the document-oriented system compares with the other systems discussed in this section.

Graph-oriented databases

Graph-oriented databases leverage graph theory from mathematics. This type of database uses concepts of nodes, edges, and properties to store information and relationships. Directed graphs are especially useful when thinking about complex relationships like schedules with multiple dependencies, or in a social network, where you need to store information about people and their connectedness. In Figure 7-3, you see how people connect to one another. For example, if this were a graph of people connected in Facebook, you can see how sending information to one person would radiate out to others.

Graph theory is the science of viewing mathematical models in terms of graphs to relate objects with one another. A social network picture is an example of a graph. Nodes are people, and the edge connects these people. The properties can define the edges, or relationships.

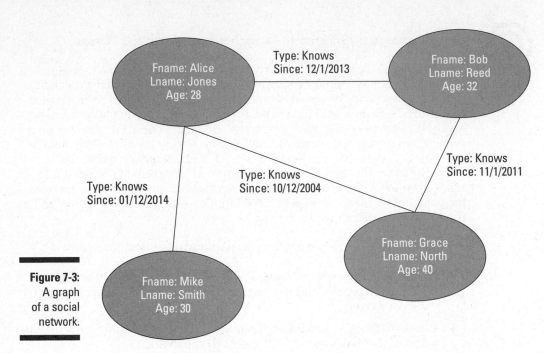

Figure 7-3:
A graph
of a social
network.

This type of database storage is especially useful for sites like LinkedIn or Facebook. We can see that the nodes are people with edges connecting those people. The properties of those edges show how they're related and for how long. Consider a project where you want to capture relationships of people from many different types of sites and see how they relate together across all social media. Storing this type of data in a traditional data store would be challenging not only for the relational connection, but in how you query that data.

One example of a popular graph technology is GraphDB (`http://neo4j.com/product`), which is used to map special data relationships call RDF Triples. The tool takes objects and facts, and graphically relates them.

Refer to Table 7-1, earlier in this chapter, for how the graph-oriented system compares with the other systems discussed in this section.

Column-oriented databases

These systems are distributed column-oriented data stores. They orient information not in rows, like traditional RDBMSs, but in columns. This allows for the natural grouping of data, which speeds up analysis.

Traditional RDBMSs must follow a very defined way to organize information called *table normalization,* which avoids repeating column types and breaks information down to an atomic nature. So, to assemble a report, a programmer has to link these atomic elements, using SQL, into groupings that make sense to a human. This can take a very long time when dealing with huge amounts of data. Traditional RDMBSs are much slower because they must make complicated and time-consuming linkages to assemble large swaths of data into reports.

Apache HBase (`http://hbase.apache.org`) is a popular distributed column-oriented data store that was modeled after Google's Bigtable system (`http://research.google.com/archive/bigtable.html`). HBase is built upon the Hadoop file system, which I cover later in this chapter. HBase allows fast access to tables that are billions of rows by millions of columns.

With column databases, you can aggregate information vertically in column families, as shown in Figure 7-4, allowing for fast access of massive amounts of data. Unlike relational models, which are row focused, large columns and summary data on those columns can be done much faster. This figure shows how a document-oriented database creates groups of things, often called *families*. Documents are detailed within these families and are stored within a column family and accessed via a key-value pair.

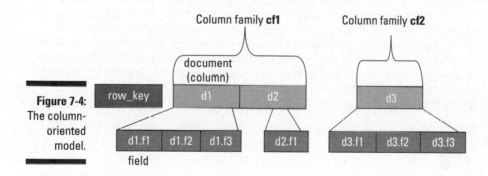

Figure 7-4:
The column-oriented model.

Big Data Framework Technologies

Aside from storing information, there are several important frameworks for organizing, accessing, and analyzing big data. In this section, I cover four important technologies that you need to be familiar with or skilled in, depending on the big data role you're pursuing.

The Hadoop framework

The Hadoop framework is an Apache open-source project — not standalone technology, but a collection of technologies. Hadoop has many implementations used by popular big data vendors like, Amazon Web Services, Cloudera, Hortonworks, and MapR.

Hadoop allows for very high-speed processing of big data by using a Map-Reduce strategy. *MapReduce* is a programming model used to process large amounts of data across parallel clustered systems. This does its workloads on files that are stored within a files system framework, like the Hadoop Distributed File System (HDFS) or even structured datasets. As you may have guessed from the name MapReduce, there are two steps in the process:

- ✔ **Mapping:** There is a master node that takes large jobs and maps those to smaller worker nodes to do the work. In some cases, a worker node could further simplify the workload to smaller nodes. (A map step is like a WHERE clause in a SQL statement.)
- ✔ **Reducing:** When the work is done by the worker nodes, the master node collects the "answers" and assembles the results. (A reduce step is like a GROUP clause in a SQL statement.)

The power is in the parallelization (working multiple jobs at the same time) of the mapping step. You can sort through petabytes of data in hours instead of days, as would be the case for traditional database queries running SQL.

The objective of Hadoop is to take lots and lots of data and derive some set of answers, or results. This is done through a map/reduce process in parallel. The data is "mapped" according to some sorting algorithm and then "reduced" through an additional summary algorithm to derive a set of results. The magic is in the parallel part. Many mapping jobs can be done at the same time across a network of computers, or *nodes*. The nodes are independent resources within a network of computer systems. By sharing the load, the job of sorting though massive amounts of data can be done quickly.

Pig

Pig and its language, Pig Latin (you can't accuse geeks of having no sense of humor), are a platform for analyzing large datasets originally created at Yahoo! for access to Hadoop clusters and later moved to the Apache open-source community. Pig Latin is the access language that is used to access the runtime environment of Pig. It's designed to make the work of creating MapReduce jobs easier. You don't have to build your own map and reduce functions, but it's another language to learn.

Hive

The challenge for traditional database programmers who move to new technologies is that they have to learn new languages and paradigms, like Pig. They've been programming in SQL for years, and moving to more pure computer science models is a challenge. Enter the Hive.

Hive allows programmers comfortable with SQL to write Hive Query Language (HQL) to query Hadoop clusters. By using a language very similar to SQL, Hive can translate SQL type calls into Hadoop-speak, which makes the usability of Hadoop much more palatable to traditional RDMBS programmers. Think of it as a translation engine. If a programmer doesn't know how to program in Hadoop, but knows how to use SQL to access data, Hive acts as that bridge and translates SQL type calls into Hadoop.

Spark

Spark is an emerging platform which is also built upon HDFS. In addition to being able to leverage HDFS, Spark can access HBase, Cassandra, and other inputs. Spark leverages grid computing for large parallel processing and can store information in RAM, which provides ultra-fast access to data and compute resources for analysis. Programmers can access Spark using Python, Scala, or Java. Spark can also be used in conjunction with graphing analytics like GraphX and MLib, which is Apache's machine learning library. The next section covers additional big data technologies like machine learning.

Analysis Tools You Should Know

In the construction industry, it's often said that the kitchen sells the house. If the end result is to communicate information to take action, then analysis and visualization tools are the kitchen of big data.

Business analytics or business intelligence tools

Business analytics (BA) or business intelligence (BI) tools can be used to directly connect to data stores, both structured and unstructured, to help in the analysis and interpretation. Appendix A fills you in on some resources for staying up to date on widely used BA and BI tools. Here are a few tools you may want to investigate:

- **Birst** (www.birst.com): Birst technologies is an on-demand, or cloud based, business intelligence and analytical tool for data analysis.

- **IBM Cognos** (www-01.ibm.com/software/analytics/cognos): Cognos is the primary product for business intelligence from IBM. It was acquired in 2008.

- ✔ **Jaspersoft** (www.jaspersoft.com): Jaspersoft is an open-source business intelligence platform.

- ✔ **MicroStrategy** (www.microstrategy.com): MicroStrategy, based in Washington, D.C., is a publicly traded business intelligence software firm that has been in business since 1989.

- ✔ **Oracle Business Intelligence** (www.oracle.com/us/solutions/business-analytics/business-intelligence/overview/index.html): Oracle has a suite of business intelligence tools, some built in-house and some acquired from Hyperion. Oracle business intelligence is a suite of tools that can work on any relational database platform.

- ✔ **Pentaho** (www.pentaho.com): Pentaho is an open-source business intelligence software firm based in Florida, in operation since 2004.

- ✔ **QlikView** (www.qlik.com): QlikView is an analytical visualization and business intelligence software firm.

- ✔ **RapidMiner** (http://rapidminer.com): Rapid Miner is tool for predictive analytics. It provides an environment for machine learning and text analytics and is offered in both a commercial and open-source model.

- ✔ **SAP** (www.sap.com): SAP is large multinational software firm based in Germany. Products like SAP HANA allow users to process and analyze big datasets.

- ✔ **Tableau** (www.tableausoftware.com): Tableau is a software firm that offers visualization and business intelligence tools.

There is a lot of debate about the terms *business analytics* (BA) and *business intelligence* (BI). Both BA tools and BI tools are used to access data, process it, analyze it, and then communicate the results to the end-user. Many vendors and pundits argue over the terms and even use them interchangeably. As of this writing, *business analytics* appears to be growing in popularity and the term *business intelligence* is receding.

Visualization tools

Not all information can be communicated in two-dimensional graphs and charts. Data can be viewed beyond the two dimensions of *X* and *Y*. When data is viewed in a third dimension, it can be connected in ways that show various relationships, patterns, and correlations.

Remember graph theory? That's where the edges and properties are applicable in a tangible way. This is where visualization tools come into play. These tools are able to communicate information, connectedness, and correlation in ways that are deep and dynamic. Data journalist David McCandless gave a famous TED talk on visualization, in which he said, "By visualizing information, we turn it into a landscape that you can explore with your eyes, a sort of information map. And when you're lost in information, an information map is kind of useful." He goes on to give some really great examples of how data visualization of big data can reveal insights that we may not have otherwise been able to understand. (You can watch the whole talk at `www.ted.com/talks/david_mccandless_the_beauty_of_data_visualization`.)

Figure 7-5 is a simple but commonly used word cloud of the U.S. Constitution. The most commonly used words are larger in size and reveal themes, trends, and main topics.

Figure 7-5:
A visualization of the U.S. Constitution.

The following is a list of great visualization tools:

- **Dygraphs** (`http://dygraphs.com`): A free JavaScript-based library for building complicated charting in web browsers.

- **Exhibit** (`www.simile-widgets.org/exhibit`): Interactive mapping tool created by MIT. Free to use.

- **Google Charts** (`https://developers.google.com/chart`): A Google-powered online charting tool.

- **jQuery Visualize** (`www.filamentgroup.com/lab/update-to-jquery-visualize-accessible-charts-with-html5-from-designing-with.html`): An open-source charting engine supporting jQuery.

✔ **Kartograph** (`http://kartograph.org`): Build interactive mapping without Google Maps that can run across any browser.

✔ **Many Eyes** (`www.ibm.com/manyeyes`): IBM-developed tools for analyzing publically available data sets.

✔ **R** (`www.r-project.org`): A free, open-source environment for graphing statistical analysis.

✔ **WolframAlpha** (`www.wolframalpha.com`): Ask this engine anything. This knowledge engine comes back with information, charts, and data. It also supports an API to programmatically retrieve charting and information.

✔ **ZingChart** (`www.zingchart.com`): A JavaScript library supporting more than 100 chart types; supports Flash or HTML5

Sentiment analysis tools

Sentiment analysis tools and processes attempt to measure how people feel about a certain thing, event, or product. Marketers like to take the pulse of people to know in near real time what a given response may be. For example, if a technology company releases a new phone product, the company may be able to measure how people feel about it by combing people's tweets, blog posts, Facebook updates, or other social media outlets.

The big data challenges include the following:

✔ **Volume:** Sifting through millions of tweets looking for relevant hashtags while mashing that up with Instagram pictures can be time-consuming to say the least.

✔ **Interpretation:** How do you interpret feeling when there is no structured way to communicate? On Twitter, spelling and grammar are almost worthless.

That's where sentiment analysis helps out. Great advances have been made in text and speech analysis, and innovation continues. But text and speech analysis aren't the only ways to measure sentiment. We can measure things like followers, retweets, likes, and other properties associated with social media moods.

There are a few levels here to consider when thinking about your place in the market. If you're a data scientist or a programmer, you can contribute to this type of technology by advancing research on text analysis, mapping human language to feeling, and building the algorithms to sort it all out.

Twitter is a common target for sentiment analysis, primarily because Twitter can give near real-time reaction to events. Other tools you can use include Google Alerts (`www.google.com/alerts`), Hootsuite (`http://hootsuite.com`), and Facebook Insights (`www.facebook.com/help/336893449723054`).

Machine learning

Machine learning is a focus within computer science that uses artificial intelligence (AI) to allow computers to automatically learn from data. A *very* simple example of this is the autocorrect or autocomplete feature on your smartphone. Your personal device "learns" the common words and phrases that you use to help with spelling correction and typing tasks. Another example is how companies like Shazam are using music data to predict the next hits by learning from historical music patterns, arrangements, and beats. Patterns emerge that tend to produce winning music formulas.

Machine learning jobs are not limited to innovative firms like Shazam. Any company that has to think about frequent user interaction and predicting future patterns can use machine learning specialists.

Keeping Current with Market Developments

You may feel as though you're hopelessly drowning in a list of technologies to tackle while new ones keep popping up. Although there is a lot to learn, you can do a few things to make sure you're staying current:

- ✔ **Don't worry about trends.** You're probably not a stock analyst, technology writer, or any other person who makes money by predicting the technology future. Don't worry too much. Settle into these foundational technologies and let the trends come to you.

  If you're interested in trends, one way to keep up with them is to join LinkedIn groups and see what others in your field are reporting.

- ✔ **Stay plugged into the community.** All the major technologies I discuss in this chapter have thriving online communities, active blogs, rich tutorials, and a glut of white papers. Find the ones you think will add value to your career path and stick to it.

✔ **Watch the innovators.** The innovative Internet companies like Amazon, Google, Yahoo!, Facebook, LinkedIn, and others have pioneered many of these technologies to enable their services for the public. They work within a very collaborative environment, and many of their contributions make it to the open-source community.

This is an exciting, dynamic, and growing field. Learning, discovery, and curiosity are core values of big data and those who aim to master it.

Part III

Finding a Job with the Right Organization

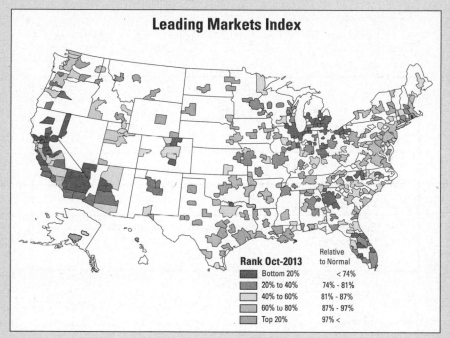

Leading Markets Index

Rank Oct-2013		Relative to Normal
	Bottom 20%	< 74%
	20% to 40%	74% - 81%
	40% to 60%	81% - 87%
	60% to 80%	87% - 97%
	Top 20%	97% <

Courtesy of the National Association of Home Builders

web extras

For more on how to start a big data team in your company, check out www.dummies.com/extras/gettingabigdatajob.

In this part . . .

- ✔ Learn what life is like within various types of organizations.
- ✔ Understand what it takes to be a consultant.
- ✔ Peak into the world of the startup.
- ✔ See how to help society through government, education, or healthcare.

Chapter 8

Life as a Consultant

onsultants. You see them in the airports, speeding through security lines like George Clooney in *Up in the Air,* jetting around the globe, and advising leaders of the most important organizations on the planet. They seem to have all the answers and hold the secrets that will make your business a huge success. If you happen to be seated next to a consultant on the plane, you'll hear stories of long hours spent in nameless towns with weeks on the road and no glory.

The truth is that life as a consultant can be all these things and more. In terms of big data career paths, the life of a consultant can take many different turns. If you're interested in pursuing this path, make sure you understand how consultants fit into an organization's strategy from both top-down planning to bottom-up execution. Consulting careers have the potential to be rewarding, both financially and intellectually. But that high reward comes with high demands. For example, you're expected to spend 80 percent of your time conducting billable hours. You can charge billable time when you're actively working on something related to your customer.

What Is a Consultant Anyway?

The word *consultant* means different things to different people. To some, it's an exalted position from which you dispense much needed wisdom. To others, it's a charlatan's trade that finds you telling people what they already know. In actuality, it's neither. As a consultant, you need to be a problem solver. You need to recognize what needs to be done to help businesses overcome pressing issues.

Types of consultants

There are two main categories within the consulting community that pretty much any consultant will fit into: management consultant and systems integrator.

The best way to look at the difference is to follow the money. Although there is some overlap between a systems integrator and a management consultant, you can usually categorize them based on where the bulk of billing revenue is derived. The systems integrator focuses on implementing an IT solution and is paid for a successful outcome. The consultant can advise about a variety of problems and can be paid for more than just one project.

Another way to look at the difference between the two is that management consultants are focused on business or the business of technology and strategy, whereas systems integrators are focused on the implantation of technology.

Management consultants

Management consultants focus on strategy and planning. They tend to operate at the executive level and address issues that have an impact on the balance sheet. Consultants who work for these firms are typically drawn from the top MBA programs globally.

Here are some common questions that management consultants are hired to answer:

- **"I've heard a lot about big data, but what does it mean to my business?"** As a management consultant, you help set the strategy and build a road map for the business leaders to capitalize on big data. You help them translate technology into business value by driving out costs or increasing revenues from the application of big data.

- **"What does big data mean for my business and how are we going to react as an organization?"** Competitors are getting big data, and as a result, the market conditions are changing. How will companies react? As a management consultant, you help companies adjust to changing market conditions.

- **"My marketing executives say they can use third-party social media data feeds to make product pricing decisions. Can we do that in our firm? What about privacy?"** Management consultants also help drive corporate policy and how companies will use customer data. Sometimes it is legal to use customer information for business purposes, but will it erode trust? Management consultants can help answer these questions.

✔ **"We need to use big data here at our company, but we have no idea where to start and what this will mean for our operational model."** Management consultants provide a strategic road map for clients to implement new initiatives. With those plans, clients can employ their people, or hire systems integrators to implement the work.

✔ **"I have an idea to start a new business unit, but I need help to operationalize the data and understand the impact it will have on the balance sheet. I need to build the business case for my executive committee."** Executives often need the help of consultants to build the business case to justify the needed investment in big data.

✔ **"We're changing how we procure and use technology for data — from hardware, software, to implementation resources and even our charge-back model. We need help to look at how we procure and finance our data strategy for the future."** Management consultants provide advice about what technology to purchase and how to finance that purchase.

Systems integrators

Systems integrators are responsible for the actual implementation work or the delivery of projects. Here are some common questions that systems integrators are hired to answer:

✔ **"We're building a big data team and need business analytics experts to help us execute."** Systems integrators can come in and shore up gaps in skills for companies.

✔ **"The CIO is supporting the marketing department on big data this year. We need help to establish best practices around data management."** Systems integrators not only provide discrete tech talent, but also can manage large projects, provide best practices, and teach their clients how to execute after they've left.

✔ **"Our IT department has no skills in Hadoop. We need a consultant for six months."** Systems integrators can provide entire project teams with skills for a fixed amount of time.

✔ **"Our firm has 60 petabytes of customer data, and we need help getting our big data team up and running."** A systems integrator can help augment the existing in-house talent.

✔ **"Our firm has released a request for proposal for a big data Center of Excellence within the company. We need a consulting firm to help us start and run that project."** Management consultants help companies write requests for proposals. These requests are sent to systems integrators to bid and are usually for very large and complex projects. Systems integrators bid on the projects with their solutions, prices, and schedules to provide solutions for clients.

Who's who in the consulting industry

Just like in any profession, some companies stand head and shoulders above the others. These are the companies that have stood the test of time and have a long trail of successes to point to. In this section, we look at companies in the consulting industry that fit that description.

Management consultants

Management consulting is great place for you to work if you want a dynamic career in big data. These jobs are highly sought after and provide access to some of the most exciting projects in the world. Within that world, technology consulting has grown more than 10 percent. This community is dominated by two groups of companies: the Big Three and the Big Four.

The Big Three includes

- **McKinsey & Company (www.mckinsey.com):** McKinsey & Company is one of the world's most trusted advisory firms. Its influence reaches across private, public, and social sectors with more than 17,000 employees in 90 offices worldwide.

- **The Boston Consulting Group (www.bcg.com):** In 2014, BCG was ranked as one of the best 100 companies to work for. It has more than 80 offices in 45 countries.

- **Bain & Company (www.bain.com):** Bain has more than 6,000 employees in 50 offices spanning 32 countries.

The Big Four includes

- **PricewaterhouseCoopers (www.pwc.com):** PwC boasts more than 184,000 employees with more than $32 billion in revenue. Like all the Big Four, tax and audit are their core business. Consulting and advisory, where big data lives, generated more than $9 billion in revenue in fiscal year 2013.

- **Deloitte (www.deloitte.com):** The largest of the Big Four with more than 200,000 professional employees, Deloitte is similar in revenue to PwC: Deloitte generated $32 billion in revenue. It has a strong consulting practice with a specialty in technology.

- **Ernst & Young (www.ey.com):** EY maintains headquarters in London. It had more than 190,000 employees worldwide and revenues of $25.8 billon in fiscal year 2013.

- **KPMG (www.kpmg.com):** KPMG, while still very large, is the smallest of the Big Four. KPMG is based in the Netherlands and had $23.4 billion in revenue fiscal year 2013.

Big data is a growing trend within all these organizations and they're building focused big data practices, which means they need more consultants at both introductory and experienced levels. In Chapter 5, we examine the types of degree programs you can pursue for a career in big data, but it's important to note that for many positions within the Big Three, consultants have undergraduate or graduate degrees in every discipline imaginable. These firms put a high priority on intellectual prowess and problem solving in their hiring methods.

Aptitude in statistics, math, and analytics is critical when working within the consulting firms that have big data practices, but your chances of landing and succeeding at interviews depends on

- **Your educational background:** Many of these firms, the Big Three in particular, are looking for candidates from prestigious schools. Consulting firms want not only great grades, but also evidence of other leadership and service outside the classroom.

- **Grade point average (GPA):** For management consulting firms, you'll be hard pressed to be considered for a first-round interview with less than a 3.6 GPA. The Big Four may not be quite as hard, but if you're in the low 3.0 range, you may be tossed out early. Good grades help to keep your options open.

- **Performance on case interviews:** How you do on case interviews is a huge part of landing jobs. Case interviews reveal how you think, solve problems, react under pressure, and display your analytical abilities. You must prepare in order perform well here. Check out Chapter 13 for more on case interviews.

Systems integrators

Years ago, there was a funny commercial advertising IBM services. The ad showed three consultants in suits with a 300-page plan for implementing new technology. The business sponsor asked when they were going to do it. The consultants looked at each other and, with a snobby laugh, replied, "We actually don't *do* anything." I'm certainly not saying that management consultants don't do anything, but when it comes to marshaling people to go about the work of implementation, companies look to systems integrators.

The systems integrator community is dominated by firms like the following:

- **Accenture (www.accenture.com):** Accenture is a worldwide consulting firm that has its roots as the technology consulting business of the now-defunct accounting firm, Arthur Andersen. Today, Accenture has more than $31 billion in revenue and more than 300,000 employees.

- **CapGemini (www.capgemini.com):** Headquartered in France, CapGemini is a multinational consulting and outsourcing company and has been in business since 1967.

- ✔ **Cognizant (www.cognizant.com):** Cognizant started as an in-house technology division of Dun & Bradstreet. It branched out and began to work for outside clients in 1994. Based in New Jersey, Cognizant has more than 170,000 employees.

- ✔ **CSC (www.csc.com):** CSC has been conducting technology consulting since 1959. It has almost $13 billion in revenue, with a significant footprint in serving the public sector.

- ✔ **Infosys (www.infosys.com):** Infosys is an India-based consulting firm serving clients worldwide.

- ✔ **TCS (www.tcs.com):** TCS has more than $14 billion in revenue, with customers in more than 40 countries. It has more than 300,000 employees worldwide.

- ✔ **Wipro (www.wipro.com):** Wipro is a publicly traded technology and outsourcing business with headquarters in India. It has more than 140,000 employees worldwide. The firm was started in 1945 as a foods company. Wipro began technology consulting in 1980 and has grown to a $7 billion business.

What about boutique or independent consulting?

Boutique consulting firms can be either management consultants or systems integrators. They're characterized by being focused on a particular discipline or industry, like marketing, financial services, or construction. Boutique firms typically have 25 or so employees. For example, GreenFrog is a small boutique firm that focuses on marketing strategies using big data for its clients. That's all it does. Its technologies, business analysts, and systems administrators focus solely on supporting the marketing departments of their clients. This is a great path for professionals who both have industry experience and big data skills and want to capitalize on their level of expertise.

To see a list of _CIO Review_'s most promising data analytics consulting companies, go to www.cioreview.com/magazine/20-Most-Promising-Data-Analytics-Consulting-Companies-ZUMY158135769.html.

Like boutique firms, _independent consulting firms_ can be either management consultants or systems integrators, depending on what they focus on: strategy or delivery. This type of firm is characterized by being a single individual with specialized contacts, industry experience, or skills. The independent is the single individual who wants to be her own boss and not have any employees. You may be reading this and thinking, "I want to be a consultant, but I don't want to work for a big firm. Is there a place for me?" The answer is "Yes!" There are thousands of people who are either independent consultants or work for boutique consulting firms. The independent consulting life is for you if you have big data skills that are in high demand and you're okay with hustling to find clients, negotiating contracts, managing the books, dealing with taxes, and actually working for your client. There is also a level of freedom involved in this type of career. You chart your own way and can choose when to work and when not to work.

This is not a complete list by anyone's standards, but these consulting firms are experts in running projects that have specific technology needs. For a current list and description of the top 20 systems integrator firms worldwide, check out *Big Data For Dummies,* by Judith Hurwitz, Alan Nugent, Dr. Fern Halper, and Marcia Kaufman (Wiley).

In addition to these systems integrators, each region has smaller firms that are attached to a group of cities or states more locally centered. This makes for less travel for the consultant and lower prices for the client.

The Career Path of a Consultant, from Associate to Partner

Career paths within consulting firms may differ from company to company, but they generally follow a prescribed path of growth based on experience, contribution, and the ability to generate fees for the firm. Consulting firms are typically organized as a partnership. The following list of titles can vary from firm to firm but they tend to follow this general pattern:

- **Associate:** Associate is the entry-level position right out of school. Associates have high analytical and business aptitude but limited experience. These people are generally hired straight out of undergrad.

- **Consultant:** Consultants have been with the firm for a few years and have grown in experience, industry knowledge, and skill. As a consultant, you gain more delivery responsibility and are in line for a leadership position. You can come on as a consultant if you come in with a master's degree in general or an MBA in particular.

- **Project leader:** This role can be multilevel. Some firms break this job out into manager and senior manager. Here, you must serve as a player-coach. You're expected to plan, deliver the work product, and lead the team. More senior-level leaders are also responsible for identifying and winning new business.

- **Principal/partner:** The top rung of the ladder is reserved for the partner. The partner shares in the profits of the practice and is often personally responsible for key clients.

As a consultant, you're there to produce fee income while building value for your client. Fee income is how consulting firms make money. When you work, you produce for the consulting firm. You also need to provide value for your clients, or your firm won't get hired to do more work and thus generate more fee income. The more experienced you are, the more you can bill.

What is experience? It's a combination of showing a successful track record and happy clients over time. Most professionals enter a consulting firm as an associate and follow the partner/principal model. The associate makes up the bulk of the workforce and often does the real work in the firm, be it as a management consultant or a systems integrator.

As an associate, you can expect that your life will be filled with a high volume of client work and career development training. People generally spend a few years as an associate and gain competencies in their area of specialty. As those skills grow, so do the areas of responsibility. Associates move to levels like senior associate, manager, and senior manager. In most firms, a senior manager (or the equivalent like a project leader) is expected to generate new revenue for the practice. This is a critical step toward gaining the coveted partner or principal position.

A Typical Day in the Life of a Big Data Consultant

What's a typical day in the life of a big data consultant? The official answer to this question (and any consulting question) is, "It depends." The following is a great snapshot taken from my experience and the life of others in the consulting world every day.

6:30 a.m. The alarm on your smartphone goes off signaling a new day. You instinctively reach for the phone to check emails and your daily schedule. You promise yourself you'll squeeze in a workout before breakfast with the team in the hotel restaurant. You worked 65 hours last week — pretty normal — but you still struggle to find time to exercise. The good news is that it's Thursday, travel home day. You and your team usually are out of town on a client project every week, Monday through Thursday.

7:30 a.m. You jump in the shower and think about what's coming up. You run through the highlights — team breakfast, internal meetings within your consulting firm, proposal work, and an executive client presentation. You need to make sure you get out of the office in time to catch your flight home. Why can't you get a project in your hometown? You remind yourself that it's just the way it goes. It'll be another full day, and somewhere in all that, you need to find time to catch up on emails, write another proposal, and contribute to a thought leadership paper your partner is writing. Your partner leads the team here at the client. You don't get to see her very often, but you know you need to perform well for her.

7:45 a.m.   Quick breakfast with your fellow consultants at the hotel. You all head over to the client's office.

8:30 a.m.   You settle into the space that you've been working out of for the past three weeks. It's an unused conference room that you and your team affectionately call the "bullpen." It can be hard to focus on writing or making calls with five people jammed into the room, but you work with what you have and you've always enjoyed a challenge. Last week you were on the 60th floor of the Willis Tower (formerly called the Sears Tower) in Chicago with a great view.

9:45 a.m.   You've reviewed the proposal, presentation, and demo that you and your team have put together. You're pitching a large big data project, which will enable a new cross-selling strategy. Though you aren't personally presenting the results to the CIO, your job is to make sure all the materials are organized. You do spot one area that you feel needs more refinement, but you can bring that up at the team meetings at 10 a.m.

10 a.m.   The five of you huddle around a phone to call the partner. You have an associate, three consultants, and the project leader (that's you). You review the materials and run through the technology demo, which showcases some emerging buying patterns based on sample data you've mined from the client's databases.

11:30 a.m.   The team meeting is over, and the team runs through the presentation.

1 p.m.   You take a late lunch with one of the direct reports of the CIO, the vice president of database platform. He is a major influencer and a supporter of your project. You've spent time over the past few months building that relationship to make sure you won't hit any unforeseen political issues in your meeting like the funding status for next year's budgets or any organization change that may be coming. Executing a big data strategy means a lot of change for your client, and the organizational impact will be large. You need to make sure you're sensitive to that and incorporate change management into your plan. Your team is recommending some changes to the staff, so you have to walk lightly.

2 p.m.   Your team is escorted into the CIO's office for the big presentation. You won't be doing the speaking, but you're there as a part of the team and to answer any questions that may come up that the partner can't answer.

4 p.m.   The proposal meeting was successful, and the client is ready to proceed to a bigger engagement and gave you a verbal agreement to move forward and start the contract process. You now have to begin building a new project team to implement the solution. You spend time with your team to discuss next steps. Some of them will move on to new projects at other clients and some will stay. You figure out who on your team may want to stay for the next phase.

4:30 p.m.   It's late in the afternoon, and you can now focus on your email inbox, which has continued to fill throughout the day. You address the emails that couldn't be handled with quick answers throughout the day from your smartphone.

6:30 p.m.   You leave the client's office to grab a cab to the airport for your 8:15 p.m. flight. Everyone flies off to their own towns. You'll work on the plane and then take late-night calls from India when you arrive at your next destination.

This snapshot is typical of life in consulting. The project specifics will vary depending on the needs of the client, however, you'll also be required to present findings, interface with executives, and keep tabs on the pulse of the client and his political adversaries.

Pros and Cons of the Consultant's Life

Consulting, whether you're a management consultant or a systems integrator, has many advantages. Consultants are always facing new challenges from different client companies, industries, and even locations. That kind of life can offer a lot of change, learning, and even high earning potential. If you pursue this life, you'll have the following advantages:

- ✔ Exposure to many different companies and industries
- ✔ The opportunity to operate at a strategic level
- ✔ High earning potential
- ✔ Experience in dealing with challenging problems
- ✔ Extensive travel

Every choice in life has trade-offs. Although you'll likely get many of the wonderful benefits of this career, there is a price. That price comes in the form of demanding hours, travel, and tight deadlines, to name a few. Check out this short list of possible downsides. Consider them carefully as you weigh you career path.

- ✔ Extensive travel
- ✔ Demanding hours
- ✔ Difficult schedules, work priorities, and deliverables
- ✔ Demanding customers
- ✔ High expectations for delivery
- ✔ A competitive work environment

ANECDOTE

High finance to consulting with big data

I believe I have a somewhat unique perspective going from a banking/high-finance background to big data/analytics at Applied Predictive Technologies (APT). My journey was both about working in big data and finding the right firm to let me use the skills I have and wanted to learn.

The summer of my third year at the University of Virginia, I interned at a major multinational investment bank, also called a bulge-bracket investment bank, in Manhattan. The internship was exciting. I loved it so much that when I came back to school I was sure I would be back, if not at that particular firm, then in investment banking. Management/strategy consulting wasn't exciting to me. I felt like the big-three consulting firms and other large consulting and strategy firms provided good opportunities to gain valuable business experience out of school, but there was a major flaw: I learned that their model was built around delivering a business case, which often centered around answering only a few analytical questions. To be sure, these were extremely complicated and deep questions, but three to six months per case seemed slow to me in this new world of big data and advanced analytics.

I only interviewed at one data-based consulting firm, APT, which I felt was an interesting gray space of critical thinking and data analytics. APT competes for the same types of candidates that traditional management and strategy

consulting firms do. APT provides consulting and strategy consulting around marketing and sales, but it has an interesting difference: APT also builds and sells a software platform that takes the analysis conducted by APT expert consultants and puts this data in the hands of clients. Instead of a fee-based model around consulting hours, APT is a software as a service (SaaS) firm.

Two things really appealed to me about APT. The ability to work across multiple projects at the same time and the data-driven analytics. True strategy consulting built off of data analytics changes the game for entry-level consultants like me. Analysis and consulting advice were no longer fueled by management's industry experience, but by data. Said another way, if you were the one analyzing the data and drawing conclusions based on the data, you also owned the analysis. This ownership and deep understanding of key business issues across multiple industries has given me a great deal of experience at a very young age.

As for how I got here, I went through the interview process: three in-person interview rounds, which included many case-style interviews. The APT website (www.joinapt.com) is a great resource to learn more about the hiring process.

—Jason Luo

Chapter 9

Working as an In-House Big Data Specialist

*E*very business today relies on technology to get work done. It's a given. You can't make cars or even serve hamburgers without technology. Enter the role of corporate IT. There are three main corporate models that firms use to serve technology to their organization: centralized IT, decentralized IT, and a hybrid approach. These models depend on several factors within a company. The advent of corporate IT came about for several reasons, including purchasing power and overall efficiency.

Imagine a company with five business units of varying size. Each business unit requires computing needs from laptops and software, to managing payroll for its employees. If each group were in charge of negotiating and buying computer hardware, software, and payroll systems, the company would have a complicated hodgepodge of technologies that would be difficult to support. Plus, if each business unit negotiated its own deal, the company wouldn't get the optimal price.

Enter corporate IT. By providing a set of shared technology services like technology procurement, networking services, and software development resources (programmers), organizations can improve efficiency for things like technical support and software development, and maximize spending through shared buying power. You may be asking yourself, "What about decentralized IT? What's that?" Depending on the maturity of the business, or the cycle that the organization is in, there would likely be an IT group within a business unit. We call this decentralized IT. In this chapter, I look at jobs within the central IT group, as well as jobs within the business units or decentralized IT.

Working for Central IT to Serve an Organization

The mission of corporate IT is to provide shared computing services to the organization. What is a shared computing service? This could be desktop support, database services, help with buying laptops to providing Internet access to a department. The idea of running a centralized IT or a decentralized IT differs from business to business. At some level, every large organization — public or private — has some sort of model for central IT services. Many groups that have centralized IT for programmers or database services will also have specialized IT needs at the departmental level. (I cover that in the next section, "Working for a Business Unit.")

Often, these roles are separated into providing application services to the business or infrastructure services, which include maintain core computing and storage services. Application services include the systems that run finance, human resources, and other systems needed to run the firm. Infrastructure services tend to be more ubiquitous in that they're viewed like a utility. If a department needs computing resources for customer software development, it can leverage infrastructure services from central IT to provide those resources.

Interestingly, many big data projects begin as shadow IT within business units. As the demand for resources grows, some of these resources shift to central IT. Shadow IT is when groups outside of corporate IT buy and run technology largely without the knowledge of IT departments.

Looking at roles in corporate IT

In the end, how centralized IT is will differ from firm to firm. The big data roles typically fall in the following categories as they relate to infrastructure or application services:

- **Infrastructure specialists:** Infrastructure specialists focus on keeping the required underlying hardware — like servers, storage, and network services — running.

- **Analytics programmers:** Analytics programmers are resident programmers who work on specific projects that may come up across different organizations within the firm.

- **Systems administrators:** Systems administrators keep the big data systems fine-tuned and running well, handle access permissions, and make sure that the latest security and software patches are installed to ensure smooth development, test, or production systems.

✔ **Systems architects:** Sometimes called enterprise architects, systems architects create the blueprints that detail how the system components will be arranged. Just like an architect of a building, these people ensure that systems are built for durability and flexibility and that they adhere to corporate standards for security.

Examining a corporate IT job posting

Following is a sample job posting for a Hadoop programmer within corporate IT. This is an actual posting for shared services within a government agency (with the name changed to protect the innocent). You can see the types of experience needed and functions required, which can give you an idea of what a day in the life of a corporate IT programmer may look like.

Senior Hadoop Developer – Health IT

Job Description

Where will you find innovation and technology?

Acme Information Systems is seeking a Senior Hadoop Developer who will analyze data for potential fraud, waste, and abuse using a variety of data analysis methods, supporting the functional requirements of a fraud prevention system, and testing the outcome of the system. This position will be located in Baltimore, Maryland and will service business units throughout the organization.

The qualified applicant will become part of Acme's information technology support services contract for the Social Security Administration (SSA).

Responsibilities for this position will include the following:

- Ensure all programming meets the standards of the production infrastructure of fraud analytics to support business unit analysts.

- Design, develop, and run analytical models.

- Work with business partners to translate business requirements into analytical models for programmers to build supporting systems.

- Assist others in understanding data as they summarize and present complex patterns of fraud in the form of easily deciphered datasets to SSA analysts.

- Perform ETL (Extract, Transform, and Load) to extract the data from multiple DBMS sources and load into SAS. Set up standard templates and coding best practices.

- Conduct data extraction that may include analyzing, reviewing, modeling, trending, and presenting information, based on provided specs, to support or refute hypotheses, leading to identification of fraud and abuse.

- Design and prepare technical specifications. Assist in project artifact documentation in business requirements documents, functional specs, flow charts. Architects design system architecture and map business needs to data requirements.

- Act as self-starter with the ability to take on complex projects and analyses independently.

Desired Skills and Experience

Basic qualifications:

- Bachelor's degree and 14 years of related experience OR 18 years of experience without a bachelor's degree

- 3 years of experience with big data analytics

- Experience with ETL tools

- Experience with open-source analytics tools like R

- 3 years of experience using Hadoop ecosystem — HDFS, MapReduce, HBase, Hive, Python, and Pig. Experience with large-scale distributed analytics platforms, databases, and reliable data movement.

There are a few things here worth calling out, starting with the specialized knowledge of this particular organization. This individual is expected to be a subject matter expert (SME) in this particular field. In this case, the level of expertise is related to the federal agency's regulatory requirements and knowledge of the enterprise architecture, which are standards the agency uses to build and deliver software applications.

In addition, this person will need to be able to work with *business customers*. This is a reference to the nature of corporate IT. **Remember:** You aren't attached to a particular line of business — instead, you serve as a "shared service" to the entire organization. This can be a really good thing if you like to stay engaged with technology and be exposed to different functions of the organization. The downside, as I explore later, is that you're a degree away from the core function of the firm.

The job also requires a significant amount of experience in related technologies. You don't simply need to know how to program Hadoop. Of course, in order to be a Hadoop developer you need knowledge of database systems and general programming knowledge. But pay attention to the vastness of the types of technologies that are required. Statistical programming (R, which is an open-source statistical programming language); database knowledge; Extract, Transform, and Load (ETL) technologies; and scripting languages like Python.

So, what are the implications of these requirements? If you're coming from a traditional programming background — say, you're a C++ or Java developer — you must be comfortable in being self-directed and working outside the confines of your "language." As you'll see in your research of big data jobs, technologies and knowledge aren't confined to one or two areas of expertise as they are in many areas of technology.

Finally, this is a senior position. This job requires a person to have 14 to 18 years of experience. It's a paradox that this role within big data, which is only a few years old, would require such experience. But this is a great example of a job function for a senior-level IT professional who is able to retool her skills for a new field. Only 3 years of big data experience is needed, but you need 14+ years of overall IT experience.

What if you don't have 14 years of experience? Flip back to Chapter 2 and see how to plan your future path.

Working for a Business Unit

Most technology jobs within a firm naturally fall within central IT, but with big data, all that has changed. Because the promise of big data is to drive new revenue, insights, and innovation, many business units have directly hired people with this expertise. Earlier in the chapter, I mention that individual business units may have specialized needs, and to that end there are in-house IT jobs that aren't a part of central IT. This is particularly true with big data.

There is a benefit to working directly within a department — you can more clearly see the fruits of your labor. You have a clear *line of sight to revenue* — your job function can be easily traced to the bottom line.

If you like being able to easily see how your work impacts the bottom line, working for a business unit is the place for you.

Just me and my shadow . . .

Shadow IT happens with a group typically within a business unit that has technology needs that central IT can't serve. There are usually three (but maybe more) reasons that it can't serve the business. Let's look at big data (of course) as an example of a very common scenario of how and why shadow IT, and eventually IT jobs within the business unit, start.

For example, maybe the marketing department of Acme has new products that have been introduced to market along with a social media campaign. Marketers want to measure the success of the release by measuring social media sentiment and mapping that to price changes, and maybe even determine if media sentiment trends will predict sales. Plus, these marketing folks may want to create dynamic pricing strategies and see how this affects sentiment in real time. To do this, the marketing department will require hardware and software to store, process, and visualize this data. In addition, it may need a lot of storage — more than the IT department has today. For them to get

this new storage, its procurement process may take six months to acquire and install — much too long for the needs of the business. These big data questions won't answer themselves, so the business team also needs specialized programmers and analysts to get things rolling. Again, as with any new technology, it isn't likely residing in central IT.

What's a manager to do? Managers often turn to cloud computing, which promises virtually limitless scalability at the push of a button. The marketing manager hires an IT professional to manage the project, hires big data consultants until she can get her own, and within a few weeks, she has a new, albeit virtual, IT department. Eventually, these jobs are so specialized to a particular business unit, that they remain within that organization, and not within corporate IT.

Again, this is a just an example but it shows how IT within a business unit is different from central IT and where it often comes from.

Pros and Cons to In-house Positions

Being the in-house big data expert — be it corporate IT or within a business unit — is a great path to consider if consulting or working for a product company isn't for you. Working directly for a company has its own unique cultural, professional, and career path consideration — both positive and negative.

Pros

Working on the inside has a lot of benefits over working for a consulting firm or a product company.

Just today, I spent time with a soon-to-be college graduate who was reflecting on her internship at a major Big 4 accounting firm (see Chapter 8). Although she really liked having diversity in her job, she felt like she didn't have a chance to go deep within her client's product offering because her projects tended to last only six weeks or so. Working directly for a company allows you to go extremely deep within that firm's business.

Here are some advantages of working for a company directly:

- ✔ **You'll have a very unique skill set within the organization.** In almost any in-house big data role, you'll be the minority even among technologists.

- ✔ **You'll have the opportunity to go very deep within an industry.** Staying put in one place gives you a chance to gain deep industry experience. This can happen as a consultant, to be sure, but it will almost always happen for in-house talent.

- ✔ **You'll be highly visible.** Big data is extremely important to driving innovation and value. Any project you work on will have a high degree of management visibility and likely high reward for success.

- ✔ **You'll have a chance to build something from the ground up.** Most big data teams within a firm are small. As such, no matter your level, you'll have a significant impact on how the team grows and matures.

Cons

Working directly for a company has its downsides. These cons are largely related to the type of culture you prefer to work in.

- ✔ **You'll be a lone wolf.** You may not be a "one-man wolf-pack" like Zach Galifianakis's character in *The Hangover,* but you'll certainly be in the minority. That means you're the expert, and career development may be a challenge.

- ✔ **You may be pigeonholed.** Some people who work within a company's IT department can feel stuck after a number of years. If you like frequent change, this may not be the place for you.

- ✔ **You have limited earning potential.** Money isn't everything, but it is important. Consultants tend to have higher earnings, so be ready for not getting compensated as much as your consulting friends.

Chapter 10

Living on the Edge with a Startup

People frequently pitch me new ideas and business plans, and I always enjoy reading them. "I have a great idea," is often how these pitches start. I've done a few startups — some succeeded and some failed. Startups have an abundance of excitement, energy, and optimism about the future — they're exciting places to be.

Many startups have emerged over the past several years that have served to provide big data tools, consulting, and services to the industry. This chapter covers the kinds of firms that are born for big data — firms whose sole purpose is to create and deliver big data solutions. This chapter also covers what life is like in a startup or early-stage company and how that contrasts to life in larger, more established firms. Finally, we explore what you can expect when looking for a job at one of these high-potential firms.

Startups and Where They Are

Startups come in all shapes and sizes and serve as the engine that allows small businesses and emerging technologies to thrive. The biggest names in global Internet and social medial companies — like Google, Amazon, and Facebook — were all relatively recent startups. Now these three firms have a combined market cap of more than $640 billion.

Startups are often *venture-backed,* where funding comes from the venture capital community. Terms like *angel investors, seed money,* and *mezzanine* are thrown around when there is talk of startups. These terms all refer to the type of funding used to fuel development, sales marketing, and growth.

Here's a list of the people and the roles they fill:

- **Core team:** These are the founders of the firm. They're the ultimate risk takers.

- **Entrepreneurial lieutenants:** These are seasoned startup individuals who have done several startups in the past. They're experts in technology, sales, and all things startup.

- **Risk takers:** These are people who may or may not have done startups in the past but are up for a challenge. They're willing to toil day and night for the payoff at the end, the fun of creation, the chance to revolutionize an industry, or all of the above.

- **Employees:** These are important people who are needed for execution, but don't usually operate well in the fuzzy space of startups.

There are five main stages of a venture-backed firm. As you read through the descriptions of each stage, think about how you like to work and which stage you think is the best fit for you.

Phase 1: The seed stage

The seed stage is characterized by small amounts of money used to get an idea off the ground to get a product or idea developed. The end result of this investment is usually some product or idea that has gotten to a stage of viability proved through customers, profits, or revenue. It could be a product that has been reviewed positively by potential clients. Perhaps an early release of a product is selling well, or the in-depth research of the seed stage is necessary to build a detailed business plan. Usually seed funding isn't enough to get the required resources needed to accelerate business growth, but it is enough to prove the idea to the initial investor community or get the interest of a broader base of investors.

Investments in the seed stage are usually quite expensive because the risk is so high. How do investors put a price on your business? Usually *valuation* (the total value of a company) is based on revenues (for growth companies) or profits (for more established firms). At the seed stage, there is usually neither revenue nor profit, so valuations are usually in the hands of the investors. They demand a high percentage of the business in exchange for cash.

If you're an entrepreneur and you're asking for $1 million, the investors will want to know what percentage of the firm you're willing to give them in exchange for that money. A 50 percent equity (ownership) stake in your firm for $1 million means that you believe your company is worth $2 million. Without revenue or a product demonstration, you certainly need to be convincing. As the value of the firm grows in later stages, the cost of capital and options for capital change as well. In my first venture-backed startup, BuildLinks, the angel investor wanted a whopping 75 percent of the firm for less than a $100,000 investment! My partner and I declined, and he later backed off his price — but that journey is for another book.

Seed funding is most often sourced from angel investors. These are usually individuals like friends, family, or other entrepreneurs. Most cities also have local investment clubs where successful entrepreneurs have pooled their money together to do seed-type funding. There are also other sources of seed funding that have no strings attached. Many regions hold case competitions, hack-a-thons, and other idea-based competitions with prize money to be used to seed the company with no equity exchange required.

Case competitions are run by various universities, interest groups, and companies to foster innovation. Participants submit ideas, products, or business plans to a panel of judges. The winner gets seed funding to start his company.

Stage 2: The early stage

When a company has already launched but hasn't been able to generate revenues to fund large-scale operations, it's considered to be in the early stage. Most firms are usually in this stage for about three years. This stage encompasses the following:

- ✔ **The startup stage:** This is the stage where an idea becomes reality. Founders coalesce around a plan to develop programs and experiment with concepts they believe in.

- ✔ **The first-round stage:** The first-round investment is usually used to fuel marketing and sales to get that the initial push for revenue. Venture capital firms will invest cash to fund further research and development and marketing or sales operations.

This is still a risky stage, and many companies stay in this world for a number of years while their product gains traction in the marketplace.

If a company struggles too many years in the early stage without growth, funding will dry up and the business will fail. For example, if the startup is a software vendor that makes a big data visualization tool, it may take years for the sales teams to penetrate large companies to gain significant traction in a competitive space. There may be a requirement of multiple rounds of venture capital investments to keep the business afloat.

Stage 3: The expansion stage

Investments received in the expansion stage help propel the company to the next level of operations. As a company grows, there is a greater need for infrastructure. Things like operations, customer service, and sales support all grow as a firm expands. Often before a company is ready to embark on an initial public offering (IPO), it will secure *bridge* or *mezzanine* funding until it raises cash on the open market.

Stage 4: The turnaround stage

The turnaround stage is one that all startups hope they will never experience. The word *turnaround* refers to the notion that the situation is bad and needs to be turned around and sent back in the right direction. There are groups who specialize in this function. They come in and assess the situation, add people who can make corrections, and help investors and employees get back on track. The solution may involve a sale or change of control.

All hands on deck

Following is a well-known example of an all-hands memo, from Fab.com CEO Jason Goldberg to employees, trying to encourage them during a turnaround.

> Have you ever been clinging onto a rocket ship, then cut the engines at full speed, and then tried to fly again? That's what we've been going through at Fab the past months.
>
> In the history of startups, I bet you can count on one hand the number of companies that went from $0 to $1 billion in valuation in just two years and then voluntarily cut their operating expenses by two-thirds and then rose to greatness again. Will Fab be able to do it? We'll see. There are days when I'm certain we will. There are days when I question if we can. I've had VC after VC tell me that they've basically assumed Fab is going to die; for how in the world can a company possibly survive three rounds of layoffs and cost cuts as we've had?

> But if there's one thing we are not going to do, it's quit.
>
> It's a @#$% startup.
>
> It's supposed to be hard. We're entrepreneurs. This is what we do.
>
> In fact, as I freely tell people, I'm actually having more fun now than ever. Why? Because we're actually doing the hard work of building a company now. We're figuring @#$% out. We're owning up to every crack and digging in and fixing it. We're fighting for our lives.
>
> If you're really into startups, this is the fun time. This is the time you earn it and learn it. Want to know what it takes to turn around a company and rebuild it? Fab is one of the only places in the world you can get that kind of experience. If you're a real startup person, this is the best time to be at Fab.

> ## Where do startups begin?
>
> So you're thinking of applying to a startup. Does that mean you need to pack your bags and move to Silicon Valley? No. Even if you don't live anywhere near Silicon Valley, odds are you're currently living in or near a thriving startup community.
>
> In 2013, the Kaufman Foundation published a study called *Tech Starts: High-Technology Business Formation and Job Creation in the United States.* Among some of the findings included was a deep-dive look into where startup activity is happening. (Note that the numbers are based on census data, which was last done in 2010.) The authors created a
>
> formula to look at the relative number of startups created relative to the population of the area. There are many interesting insights in the study, but the main point is that not everything is centered around San Francisco. The encouraging news from the study is that in 2010 there were 78 metro areas with significant startup densities.
>
> You can download the full report at `www.kauffman.org/what-we-do/research/firm-formation-and-growth-series/tech-starts-hightechnology-business-formation-and-job-creation-in-the-united-states`.

Stage 5: The purchase stage

If the startup has successfully moved from the seed stage to the expansion stage, there is a chance that investors will want to purchase the company outright. These investors are betting on the idea that with a transfusion of cash they can make the company larger and more profitable. At this stage, the founders either cash in and move on or try to cut a deal that includes them in the new phase.

Startup Companies Born for Big Data

If you're going to work for a company dedicated to big data, it will almost have to be a startup. Why? Because of the newness of the field.

However, with the advent of cloud computing, people can more easily build companies with much less capital expense and valuable resources focused on building technology infrastructures. Where many employees used to be required, today companies can create a massively scalable data center using just a credit card. The cloud has truly transformed not only enterprise computing but the capability for small companies to innovate and scale out with the power that was only available to the largest companies.

Getting connected to the startup scene

You can get connected to the startup scene in your area in a few important ways. These vary by city but most cities have both formal and informal opportunities to connect. Use the web to search for startup group meetings to exchange ideas, concepts, and war stories. For example, there are several pitch night groups that host meetings to connect angel investors, venture capitalists, and entrepreneurs. In towns with major universities, you can find hack-a-thons sponsored by big companies, startups, and venture capital firms. When you start investing your time in these groups, you'll quickly find ways to get connected to the next big thing and find that next big job in big data.

There are three main categories of startup firms where you'll typically find employment in the big data space:

- **Independent software vendors:** These are software vendors building tools for big data access, collection, storage, analysis, or data visualization. There is some risk involved in joining a company like this unless it is profitable and has a track record to point to.

- **Big data software as a service (SaaS) providers:** SaaS providers are companies that provide access to big data tools via web services. These companies are often well established and have long-term clients. If this is the case, there is less risk in joining them. However, there is more competition for a job like this.

- **Consulting firms:** Large companies will continue to invest in big data but will rely on big data experts to implement big data in-house.

 A potential opportunity you may want to consider is getting a job at a digital marketing company. Many digital marketing companies are building big data practices out of necessity. Their customers are running big data projects and are asking their agencies to manage these big data projects along with their typical marketing campaigns. If you're interested in marrying marketing and big data, this could be a good avenue for you.

Deciding If Working for a Startup Is the Life for You

Life in the startup world requires employees to be ready for a few things that are outside their normal job function. There is no IT department to help you when your laptop is broken. Well, actually there is — you. The concept of normal hours goes out the window and what you do day to day depends on the needs of the business. Some of these shifts may be exciting! But if you like predictability and consistency, your days and nights will be filled with tension.

Here are some of the advantages of working for a startup:

- **High earning potential:** Though pay is usually low, many employees are compensated with stock options. That may not seem like much right now, but ask early AOL employees how they feel about stock options today.

- **New challenges every day:** No day is the same. Because technology changes rapidly, so do the business goals. This can make for an exciting day or one that is filled with chaos and unpredictable hours.

- **Opportunity to influence change:** If you have a good idea, you'll be heard and you'll have a chance to do something about it. You'll also build your résumé and secure the future of your career.

On the flip side, here are some drawbacks to working for a startup:

- **No life outside work:** Startup teams are expected to work long hours to deliver projects and services no matter what. When you hear about all those cool toys at a startups — like pool tables, beer kegs, and sleeping cots — remember that those are there because the employees are basically living in the office. Forget about having a life outside work when you work for a startup. It doesn't exist.

- **Low pay:** Startups are notoriously low paying in the short term. People get involved in startups either because they believe in the idea or because they're hoping the company will be bought by an industry giant that will pay them handsomely.

- **Lack of job security:** You could lose your job with little warning. There are no guarantees. Founders can give up and move on at a moment's notice. Another possibility is that other people can be brought in who can do your job better and you're out.

- **High stress:** The stress levels are high during almost every phase of the life of a startup. The pressure to innovate and deliver sales and product never ends. Expectations are sky high from investors and customers alike.

Chapter 11

Serving in the Public Sector or Academia

. . . .

In This Chapter

▶ Learning about life in academia

▶ Looking at public sector big data responsibilities

▶ Identifying big data roles that impact healthcare

. . . .

*N*ot all the jobs in big data are concerned with driving profits or revenue. Many roles in big data out there are in the public sector or university settings working toward public safety, medical discovery, and the advancement of science. Instead of looking for the best pricing combination or executing a online shopping basket analysis, you may find yourself wanting to uncover future signs of cancer, predict where the next disease may strike, or run simulations on clinical trials to find a cure for a disease.

This chapter covers the role big data plays in different areas of the government, how higher education leverages big data, and how you can explore the job possibilities.

The Role of Academia in Advancing Big Data

Higher education plays a very important role in the big data ecosystem. From training new talent to pushing the envelope of innovation, there are many exciting areas available for people interested in big data careers.

Teaching at the college level

The foundation of academia is teaching. The role of the university is critical for teaching the next crop of mathematicians, scientists, and business analysts. If you're considering a role as a professor, you'll find big data to be a very rewarding and challenging field.

Here's the typical career path of a college professor after earning a PhD:

- ✔ **Assistant professor:** The role of assistant professor is for newly minted PhDs. It's an entry-level job at a university or college that puts the professor on a tenure track. If the professor doesn't rise to the rank of associate professor within eight years, he's usually dismissed.

  Tenure is a status that is granted to select professors guaranteeing them employment after they complete a probationary period. Professors are tenured to ensure that they won't lose their jobs because of political infighting or other nonteaching issues. Tenure provides them the academic freedom to teach in their own way without fear of repercussions.

- ✔ **Associate professor:** The role of associate professor is the next step up toward tenure from assistant professor. Associate professors are generally experienced academic researchers. Not all associate professors are on a tenure track. Those who aren't may remain at this level and won't go on to gain tenure.

- ✔ **Full professor:** Professors who have risen through the ranks from assistant professor to associate professor are promoted to full professor. Full professors are very senior members of the faculty and have tenured positions.

- ✔ **Endowed chair:** Endowed chairs, sometimes called distinguished professorships, are honorary positions linked to an endowment that funds the person's salary. You know these individuals because they have titles like one of my colleagues at the University of Virginia, Thomas Bateman, Bank of America Eminent Scholar, Professor of Commerce. That's a mouthful!

Though the academic path is straightforward, it isn't easy or automatic. In most cases, when an assistant or associate professor is being considered for the next level, everything is on the line. If tenure isn't granted, he's often dismissed from the university. Competition is tight, pressure to publish is high, and strong performance in the classroom counts. Remember those surveys you used to fill out at the end of a class? Those are used for the professor's career progress.

What about your buddy at work who also teaches a class at the local university? You can be that person, too. There is a class of educators at the university level who are not on the formal professor track. They might be called lecturers or adjunct professors. These titles are reserved for part-time faculty members who are at the university for teaching purposes and usually have other jobs. They don't usually have the research or service requirements that other faculty members have — they're focused on classroom teaching. All schools, from the largest universities to the smallest community colleges, employ part-time faculty to help meet classroom demand or bring in professionals with specialized knowledge to add value to their programs.

Conducting research

Universities are centers for research. When you think of research, you may imagine lab coats, bubbling beakers, and Bunsen burners. But much of the research that is conducted today is focused on data analysis. There are a variety of research jobs in universities — from research assistants all the way to post-doctorate researchers. These roles are often funded through grants from the National Science Foundation, the Department of Energy, the Department of Defense, the National Institutes of Health, and many other agencies in conjunction with university research. Some of the positions may last only as long as the funding lasts.

Nonprofit Industry Organizations

Nonprofit organizations often serve an entire industry as a whole. They're funded by member companies to drive the following:

- **Big data research:** Some groups fund projects to explore new areas in big data. These funds can be used to conduct research new software in big data or ways to apply the technology.

- **Technology standards:** As industries develop, there is a growing need for people to agree on a common set of ways to exchange information, define terms, and integrate systems. It's like grammar for a language. When a group can agree on the rules of how words should work, it makes it much easier to communicate.

- **Awareness:** These groups conduct events, conferences, or publications to promote general awareness of big data technology.

Companies and organizations often come together to build information and data systems that all member firms may benefit from, even though they're competitors in some cases. For example, The Data Warehouse Institute (http://tdwi.org) is made up of members from competing firms. However, they collaborate to promote the industry as a whole.

Another example is the National Association of Homebuilders (NAHB), an organization that has been around for more than 70 years and has 140,000 member firms. Homebuilding represents a huge part of the U.S. gross domestic product (GDP) when you factor in all the associated trades and industries. Data, insights, and research from the NAHB impacts financial markets, public policy, building and safety standards, and a number of other key issues. Figure 11-1 shows a heat map representing the leading building markets in the United States to illustrate the new construction housing recovery. Heat maps show concentrations, or heat, of groups of data by a concentration of a particular color.

Leading Markets Index

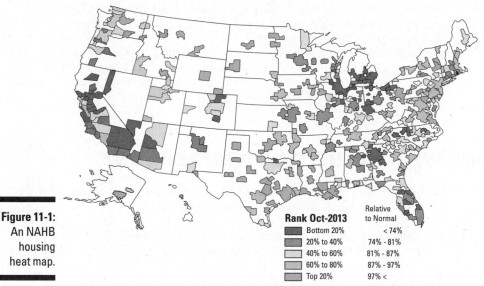

Figure 11-1: An NAHB housing heat map.

Rank Oct-2013	Relative to Normal
Bottom 20%	< 74%
20% to 40%	74% - 81%
40% to 60%	81% - 87%
60% to 80%	87% - 97%
Top 20%	97% <

Courtesy of the National Association of Home Builders

Organizations within the Public Sector

Public sector jobs are typically segregated into civilian and defense. Their customers are the agencies or organizations they're tasked to serve. These groups can be local, state, or federal. Public sector jobs are focused on supporting infrastructure, services, public safety, and regulatory needs. For example, in public safety, you may analyze crime data to predict where to apply funding for a police force, or you may analyze disease data to help provide input for policymakers and lawmakers. The insights from big data can have a huge impact on the government.

McKinsey & Company, a management consulting firm, has identified three major areas for the uses of big data in public sector administration:

✔ **Operational efficiency:** Gaining savings by identifying better ways to get things done.

✔ **Reduction and prevention of fraud:** Helping to spot abuse and fraud by identifying patterns in claims, whether medical benefits or tax returns.

✔ **Increased tax revenue collection:** Finding where to apply regulations to help increase tax revenues by identifying tax gaps in businesses and individuals.

Big data can also be used to predict potential crime networks, terror connections, and other crime risks. Big data analysis can be used to spot and predict health and disease information that can be used by policymakers who are appropriating funding for medical research.

Another useful way that the federal government can use big data is to find ways to reduce taxes and to spend tax dollars more efficiently.

Civilian organizations

Civilian organizations are local, state, and federal government groups that are not associated with defense and intelligence. These include law enforcement groups like the local police and the Federal Bureau of Investigation (FBI), which is a part of the Department of Justice.

Life in these groups differs vastly from one agency to the next, but they do share a lot of the same characteristics:

✔ **The application processes are tightly regulated.** It isn't as easy as calling your buddy who does the hiring. Public organizations generally have many applicants and need to follow a fair and regulated process.

✔ **The pay scales will likely be less than in the private sector.** Raises are often at the mercy of the local economy, state governor, or organizational head.

✔ **Most of these groups have appealing retirement plans for those who are able to participate.** This long-term security can be worth a bit of lower pay during your career.

Somebody once said that steady plodding brings prosperity. So if you're inclined to leverage your skills for the benefit of society, the public sector could be a great fit!

Defense and intelligence

Some government agencies have been leveraging big data to run analytics to identify potential threats to the United States. These threats include such things as spying from foreign countries, attacks to our financial institutions, and cyber-terrorism. The task of sifting through unstructured data like voice files (which could include recorded phones calls or voicemails) and emails in search of patterns to identify future threats is a classic case of using big data.

Consider an example of government intelligence agencies that need to isolate events related to suspected conversations related to terrorist activities. These events can occur via emails, text, voice, and other media. The first step would be to isolate noise from the relevant content, creating a group of interest. With big data, agencies can

- ✔ Identify potential terrorist threats in near real-time by running action-able advanced analytics on all available data.

- ✔ Aggregate critical data from disparate sources in real-time including documents, email, audio and video files, social media posts, and blogs.

- ✔ Perform behavioral analysis to isolate risk and threats, and understand behavior within and among groups.

- ✔ Build targeted identification campaigns for specific suspect segments.

- ✔ Perform suspect behavior analysis to predict potential threats and antic-ipate suspects' behavior and movements.

- ✔ Communicate real-time decisions and desirable actions effectively among all impacted persons and emergency personnel.

Given the technical and data requirements, you can see that government agencies have a high demand for big data analysts. People who enter a three-letter agency like the FBI, Central Intelligence Agency (CIA), National Security Agency (NSA), and Defense Intelligence Agency (DIA), enter at a rank structure somewhat similar to the military. There are job classifications that determine the level of responsibility and associated pay grades.

You hear these letters in the news, books, and movies, but what do they mean and what do they do? Here's a quick rundown:

- ✔ **CIA:** The CIA's main purpose is to gather information on foreign governments, firms, or people, and provide that information to U.S. policymakers. Big data jobs can be used to analyze information to help predict where the next threat to the United States may come from.

✔ **DIA:** The DIA is similar to the CIA, but it focuses on foreign military capabilities. Big data jobs are focused on data analysis of information related to military operations.

✔ **FBI:** The FBI is the U.S. Department of Justice's group to investigate crimes on behalf of the federal government. This includes organized crime, terror, and other federal crimes.

✔ **NSA:** The NSA's main goal is to monitor global communication for intelligence gathering and to protect the U.S. communication capability.

Figure 11-2 shows a posting taken from www.cia.gov for a data scientist within the agency. As you can see from this posting, the salary range is quite wide and depends totally on your experience level. Much of the work is similar to a corporate IT job within the commercial sector. The main difference is that the objective of the analysis involves national defense instead of assisting business units in increasing profitability.

Data Scientist
Work Schedule: Full Time
Salary: $51,934 – $138,136
Location: Washington, DC metropolitan area
Positions available range from entry level to full performance.

Do you have a passion for creating data-driven solutions to the world's most difficult problems? The CIA needs technically-savvy specialists to organize and interpret Big Data to inform US decision makers, drive successful operations, and shape CIA technology and resource investments. The CIA is looking for individuals from diverse educational backgrounds to fill the role of data scientist. If you have experience in data analytics, computer science, mathematics, statistics, economics, operations research, computational social science, quantitative finance, engineering or other data analysis fields, consider a career as a Data Scientist at CIA.

As a Data Scientist at CIA you will get to work with advanced hardware, software, and techniques to develop computational algorithms and statistical methods that find patterns and relationships in large volumes of data. Through CIA's global mission, the agency has access to unique data sets that can be analyzed in one computational environment. Successful applicants will have keen technical insight, creativity, initiative, and a curious mind.

Data Scientists will be expected to communicate their conclusions clearly to a lay audience and become experts through continued education, attending academic and technical conferences, and collaboration with the Intelligence Community.

Qualifications:
Entry Level: Bachelor's degree and experience with applied quantitative research working with real world data, either through thesis research, internships, or work experience. Applicants should have demonstrated creativity, initiative, and leadership abilities.

Developmental: A Bachelor's or Master's degree and 2-5 years of work experience in a Data Science equivalent field or sub-field, working with data rich problems either through research or programs and experience with computer programming. Applicants should have demonstrated ability to successfully complete projects with large or incomplete data sets and be able to provide solutions.

Full Performance: A Master's degree, or equivalent work experience, and 5+ years experience in a field where you have applied technical methods to a substantive problem. Applicants should be an expert in their field and have demonstrated ability leading Interdisciplinary teams throughout the full course of a project's life-cycle.

Minimum Requirements: A Bachelor's degree with a GPA of 3.0 or better on a 4.0 scale as well as initiative, creativity, integrity, technical excellence and strong interpersonal and communication skills. A self-starter attitude, the ability to work independently and in a group, demonstrated initiative, and writing/briefing skills are also required.

Figure 11-2:
A posting for a data scientist job at the CIA.

Healthcare and Medical Research

McKinsey & Company is a prestigious consulting firm that works with leaders in business and government around the world. It made a huge impact in the world of big data with some very big claims in its 2011 report, *Big Data: The Next Frontier for Innovation, Competition, and Productivity*. McKinsey projected the impact of big data on healthcare in the United States could top $300 billion per year, which is more than double the total annual health spending of Spain.

Using information to improve healthcare is in the infancy stages today, which should bode well for the future of big data job growth. There are three factors to support this:

- ✔ The increase of digital usage for patients like electronic medical records.

- ✔ The lack of integration that exists today across healthcare providers, payers, governments, and drug companies.

- ✔ The amount of data that will result from the increase in usage of complex data systems from research to treatment.

Healthcare companies need to derive insights from the data they collect, but this is complicated by a lack of system integration. This lack of integration is only an opportunity for growth in jobs, responsibility, and innovation. This means that big data people entering the workforce today will be part of a huge movement to bring massive advancement across this complex network. There is great room for innovation when gaps like this exist.

You may wonder what this means for big data? This leads us to the final factor that promises huge job potential for big data workers in the near future and long term. With millions of people using digital devices within their healthcare network, there will be an enormous glut of data from which we can pull untold insights. I say "untold" here, because we just don't fully understand what will be discovered. That is the big promise of big data!

Part IV
Developing a Job-Landing Strategy

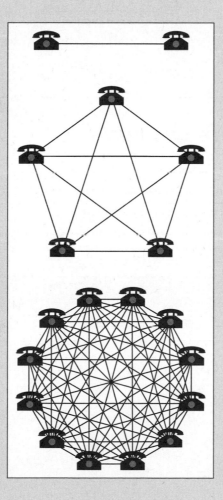

For more how to prepare for a case interview, check out www.dummies.com/extras/gettingabigdatajob.

In this part . . .

✔ Learn how to put your tools into action

✔ Leverage your networks, both real and virtual.

✔ Write a résumé to get noticed for big data.

✔ Discover what to expect in an interview and learn how to prepare for one.

Chapter 12

Building Your Network and Brand

*P*repare your résumé, apply online, and the jobs will roll in, right? Well maybe . . . but probably not. Finding a job today has many dimensions beyond the résumé and online job application. They include proper education, skills, experience, and something that is increasingly important in today's job market: a personal brand. Understanding how to build an online brand is key to standing out among all the other voices clamoring to be heard.

Before you run out and hire a public relations consultant, you can do a few simple things to make your brand more visible and make yourself more attractive to potential recruiters and employers. Beyond combing the job boards and career pages of the organizations you want to target, there are two main channels to explore: online social brand management and real-life, look-'em-in-the-eye human connections. In this chapter, I connect the two with a guide to build your online brand and grab the attention of the employers you want to work for.

Real-World Networking to Win a Job

Do you have a friend who always seems to do a good job of keeping in touch or seems to know someone everywhere he goes? People like that appear to be naturals at networking. Like anything in life, for some networking comes naturally — but it's a skill that can also be cultivated.

 Human connections — whether face to face or over the phone — are still the foundation for landing a great job. The connections you cultivate now will often pay dividends in years to come in ways that you can't predict. You reap what you sow. Take the time to plant seeds today, and you'll harvest valuable connections in the future.

Your short-term goal is to get connected to real people who can either hire you or get you a step or two closer to someone who *can*. Your long-term goal is to create a solid base of connections that you can both support and leverage for years to come as your career develops. Networking is a two-way street — you can't just ask people for support and assistance without being willing to do the same in return.

Many networking connections are one-way — "Connect with me because I need something from you." This kind of request usually falls on deaf ears. A good way to make a new connection with someone is to ask for feedback. One question you can ask to get started is, "Can I get a moment of your time to get your opinion about how you see big data fitting in your industry?" People like be asked to give their opinion. If you ask for help and be specific, you're more likely to get a response than if you just ask for a meeting without a clear agenda.

Knowing where to look

So, how can you find the right people to network with? Networking is hard enough without wasting time in places that aren't conducive to interaction with other business people. The best way to get started is to find groups that are composed of people who work in your industry.

Industry interest groups

An *industry interest group* is a group of likeminded people who meet in person to discuss ideas, promote new thinking, and make connections. Groups like this exist in many forms, ranging from formal conferences to information meet-ups that are initially organized online.

Many cities or regions have nonprofit organizations that are meant to promote technology development, research, and business in the region. These groups are sponsored by businesses and government programs and offer membership, conferences, and great opportunities to get plugged in to the technology culture in the community. To find these kinds of groups in your area start by firing up Google and searching for "groups *<industry> <your local area>*" (for example, "groups big data New Jersey"). Try that and see all the groups you instantly find in your area.

Other great places to connect include the following:

✔ **Conferences:** There are national and local conferences on Hadoop, Apache, Spark, and other technologies in big data. Conferences offer opportunities to connect with other people in the industry; plus, you can hear major influencers talk about important topics in big data and supporting technology. Check out Appendix A for some conferences I recommend.

- **Trade shows:** The main purpose of trade shows is to market products and services. Many emerging vendors have key leaders in the booths or leading talks and sessions. Attend these trade shows. Listen, learn, and connect. Check out Appendix A for some trade shows I recommend.

- **Vendor summits:** Most vendors sponsor global, national, and regional conferences solely focused on their technologies. A summit is similar to a conference, but a summit is much more focused on a particular suite of products or solutions.

- **Meet-ups:** Open an account at Meetup (www.meetup.com), and search for a big data group to connect with. If there isn't one in your area, start it! You can prepare an agenda, get feedback from interested parties, and then hold a meeting that promises to provide lots of good networking opportunities. You may want to invite a speaker to your first event so that she can help bring in new members among her following.

Alumni networks

As the old saying goes, "It's easier to farm than to hunt." In other words, you likely already have rich networks in place today from your alma mater. Universities offer several great ways to leverage the alumni network:

- **Alumni database:** Virtually every school's career services or alumni group has a database accessible to alums. This database is a rich source of potential contacts for prospecting for that next job.

- **Career services:** Even if you've already graduated, many career services departments are more than willing to help you in your search and make connections for you. After all, if you get a great job, your university looks better! Contact your university's career services office, and ask what kinds of resources they have available.

- **Alumni associations:** Alumni associations aren't just about giving money and getting sweet seats at next year's football games. Many universities have chapters all around the country and are quite active. Local alumni chapters are great places to make important connections that can last a lifetime. Check out your local alumni chapter for meet-ups and networking events.

- **University lifelong learning:** Universities often sponsor lecture series for prominent alumni to come and speak. Some also offer alumni field trips. For example, the McIntire School of Commerce at the University of Virginia sponsored a trip for alumni to visit Capital One's Innovation Lab in the Washington, D.C., area. There, alumni got the chance to hear about innovations Capital One was making in big data, analytics, and technology. Alumni from all professional levels attended, making the event a great opportunity for networking!

If you've been in the workforce for more than a few years, you have a great built-in network of former colleagues. You can most likely find them on LinkedIn. If you get laid off, your human resources department may provide services or coaches for getting connected to the next job opportunity.

Being ready to make that connection

When you're on the hunt for a new job, you need to always be ready to ask for the opportunity if it presents itself. Now, I'm not saying you should have your résumé folded up in your coat pocket at all times, but you should be prepared to engage when the opportunity arises — and you never know when that'll happen.

There are some tips to keep in mind so that you can take advantage of the moment when it presents itself:

- **Have a story and be ready to tell it.** This is a big one. Personal narratives are important. Spend some time thinking about your personal narrative. Whole books have been written on this topic. As Stephen Covey wrote in *7 Habits of Highly Effective People,* think about your story in terms of what you want to *be,* not what you want to *do.*

  To build your story, ask yourself the following questions:

    - Is your current circumstance a part of your plan, or were you forced to make a change?

    - If you didn't plan on this defining moment in your life, how are you reacting to it?

    - What do you want your story to be in five years?

  Think about where you've come from and where you're going. Write your story well and with purpose. Employers are interested in people who have a plan and a purpose, people who are introspective.

- **Be real.** When you're talking to someone about your skills or what you've done, don't falsely inflate your background. You won't fool anyone — you'll only turn them off. It's okay to talk about your accomplishments, but strive to be humble.

- **Be discerning.** Not everyone you meet lives by the "be real" principle. Learn to discern when people are inflating their own importance. If this is happening, you know that this contact is likely not worth your time for two reasons:

    - He's probably not someone you want to work with.

    - He's likely overstating his ability to get you a job.

- **Get to the point.** Don't overengage with details or information. You're very interesting to you, but chances are that others may not share the same level of enthusiasm. Again, be humble.

- **Ask for a meeting.** If you've found someone who has influence over hiring, ask for a meeting. Even informational interviews can open up opportunities.

ANECDOTE

A lesson in job hunting

After my first year of college, the job market was tough, but I knew having experience working with a technology company would really help me in my education, boost my résumé, and validate that I wanted to work in that field for the long term. Internships aren't easy to get when you're early in your college career, but I was able to land one. There are some valuable lessons I learned in landing that internship. First, don't assume anything — just because you don't have all the qualifications for a job, doesn't mean you shouldn't try. Second, listen to wise counsel; in my case, it was my dad. Finally, follow up — that's what got me my job!

I was finishing up my freshman year of college. In January, my dad encouraged me to start thinking about a summer internship. I thought an internship might be impossible because most internships went to seniors, and some juniors, but certainly not freshmen. I went down to career services to look through the summer job postings and my concerns were confirmed. I didn't have a lot of schooling under my belt, but I knew I was analytical, hardworking, and had high aptitude to learn on the job. Unfortunately, there aren't a lot of jobs asking for just those things. I decided that I wasn't going to assume the only way to get a job was through the traditional channel. My dad encouraged me to go directly to the places I wanted to work and plead my case, *even if they didn't have jobs posted*. Don't assume they aren't hiring. That turned out to be a great idea!

I was living in Richmond, Virginia, so I targeted all the companies in Richmond that fit my field. This was before the Internet was pervasive, so

I had to pull out the phone books, talk to friends, and network with people face to face (crazy, I know). I made a list of the firms I wanted to work for in the region. I prepared my résumé and sent them unsolicited, with a cover letter explaining why I would be a great summer hire. As time went on, I got rejection letters back or heard "No, we aren't hiring" when I called. My dad encouraged me to keep pushing and take another angle. So I did.

I decided that I would continue to send my résumés and cover letters, but I needed to do something more to stand out. After I mailed my package, I decided to go to the office and ask for a meeting with the most senior person. That turned out to be a great strategy. Early in the spring, I saw a firm that I thought would be a great place to work and gain experience. They didn't actively recruit at my school and they weren't advertising for summer interns. That was okay with me, I wanted a job. So, I did the usual mailing, but this time I followed up with an office visit. I found a senior partner there who was available to give me an informational interview and talk about the firm. I told him that I wanted to work there for the summer and asked if he'd consider bringing me on. He did! The best part of the story happened when I returned home. There was a letter waiting for me in the kitchen from this firm. I opened it up and found a rejection notice, saying that they weren't hiring. Had I not gone in person, I would've taken that rejection like all the others and had no job. I learned to think about my career pursuits with creativity and perseverance, and to focus on follow up.

—Susan Williamson

Building Your Brand While Networking

Sharpening your personal brand through real-world and online connections is difficult. If any of this seems a bit overwhelming, don't worry. This section will break down some brand-building strategies to get you rolling. This five-step process will help you tackle the process.

Step 1: Define your goals

I'm a strong advocate of setting goals and metrics to measure success. Ultimately, your goal is to land a job, of course. But let's take it a bit further. Maybe your goal is to be better connected to the local startup or small business community. Perhaps you want to be known as the go-to person for a particular technology, method, or aspect of big data.

Write down your goal, and figure out some metric to decide if you've achieved it. For example, maybe you want to be viewed as an expert in Spark as well as sentiment analysis. You can define some metrics to track this goal by the kind of hits you're getting on LinkedIn or job sites. Does 50 hits a day mean people think you're an expert? No, but it is one dimension.

A defined, written goal gives you something tangible to look at and work toward. And it keeps you motivated!

Step 2: List your current networks

Make a list of your current active and relevant networks. Those could include university, fraternity/sorority, military, or community networks, as well as any social media networks you're part of. List those networks that are the most valuable — the ones where you have the most connections.

Many people overlook the people who surround them every day. Make sure you're well connected to people in your own team, in your department, and in other departments in your organization.

Networks are more valuable with more nodes. According to Metcalfe's Law, illustrated in Figure 12-1, the more nodes a network has, the more potential value there is.

In Figure 12-1, you can see that two telephones make one connection. Five telephones makes ten connections. And 12 phones makes 66 connections!

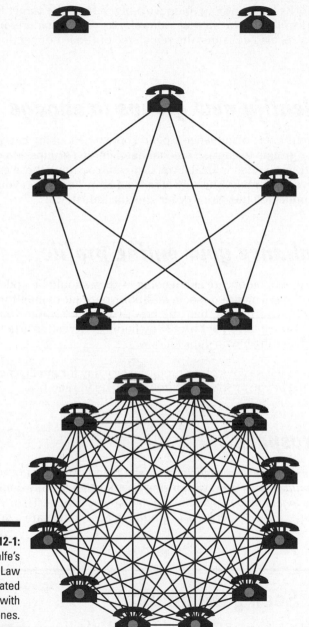

If your best networks have nothing to do with big data or the target industry, those networks may not be all that valuable. As you consider your current network size, also consider the relevance of those connections to your goals.

Step 3: Identify new groups to engage

Expand your current circle of influence. Spend some time looking in your local resources for groups to engage. I recommend finding groups and organizations on the national, state, or local level. List why you think these groups are important so you can rank your networks from Step 2 based on your priorities and how connected they are to your specific industry.

Step 4: Enhance your online profile

Online profiles require a bit of care and feeding — they should be updated or at least checked every month or so. In addition you want to monitor your profiles every day to determine if there are new people with whom you can connect. You can also enhance your profile by finding interesting articles and industry news and sharing it with your followers.

Check LinkedIn and your various other profiles every day for intelligence about who is looking at you or where you're coming up in searches.

Step 5: Prospect

Conduct online job searches, engage your network, and prospect not only for jobs but for key *people* associated with hiring for those jobs. For example, look at the groups available on LinkedIn and join some of them. Then you can reach out to specific members of the group because you share a group in common.

Seeing the future

Many years ago, in the early 2000s, I was sitting in a bar with friends and we were debating if all the shopping malls, big box stores (like Walmart and Target), and grocery stores were going to go out of business. Half of us thought that this thing called the World Wide Web would change everything; the other half thought it was a fad. I was in the camp that believed that the Internet would change everything. Granted, I was a bit extreme in my thinking. In fact, I believed that within three years, we would all be locked in our homes, no one would ever go to an office again, and all our food, books, and movies would be delivered by robots. A year later, everything had crashed, and a year after that, people started talking about Google, Amazon, and eBay. I came full circle after the market crash, and I told people that those companies were in their death throes and would be gone in six months. In short, I took little action to benefit from the huge wave of opportunity that stood before us. I missed out.

Two years ago, a friend of mine told me about his new job with a leading Hadoop platform company, which was in startup mode. In many ways, I thought that this was just the same trend with different technology. I didn't want to take interest. At first, my friend said that this world of Hadoop and big data was the greatest thing since the inception of the search engine. Six months later, he told me he might have to find a new job. He said, "Everyone wants to talk about this, but no one wants to buy it." Well, the wave of big data continued to gain momentum and just a few months ago, he told me that he had closed a staggering number of deals and that he would make more money he had ever dreamed possible. This doesn't even include the stock options he had garnered as an early employee, which is very common in software companies.

The question I had was, "Will I sit idly by, or will I take action now?" For me the choice is clear, and I'm feverishly focused on cracking my way into this space. I didn't get in as early as I would have liked to, but I believe that there this still a great window ahead of us where fortunes will be made and businesses will be transformed. I'll will damned I if I let this type of opportunity slip by a second time.

The next question I asked myself was, "How am I going to crack into this space?" I looked at my assets and one of the most valuable thing I have is my network. I'm now actively engaged with a number of leaders in the space. I leveraged research on LinkedIn and other networking sites to see what connections I could make. For example, with just a few phone calls and an email, based on relationships I see on LinkedIn, I've been able to gain contacts with some of the leading big data and cloud companies.

Using my social and business networks has been absolutely key for me in two areas. First, it's given me the chance to identify what companies I really want to work for. They publish articles, research, and information about what they're doing. Second, I can determine what my relationship is to people I want to talk to within the companies I want to work for. I then use those connections to gain access to those leaders.

Maybe we won't be locked in our houses waiting for robots to do everything for us (wait, did I just see a drone fly by?), but I've certainly come to realize that big data and social networking aren't fads — they're a part of how we do business.

—Richard Savage

Chapter 13

Creating a Winning Résumé

In This Chapter

▶ Defining the purpose of a résumé within the hiring process

▶ Learning the keys to good résumé writing

▶ Examining both good and bad résumé elements

*W*riting a good résumé is the initial entry point into most quality employment opportunities, yet so many people fail to write a compelling résumé and take advantage of those opportunities. In theory, writing a résumé shouldn't be difficult because you're writing about someone you know very well: Yourself! Unfortunately, many people fail because they don't understand the role of the résumé, they don't know what message to deliver in their writing, or they fall into the trap of omitting good information and emphasizing bad information.

In this chapter, I explore the role of résumés in the hiring process and why a good résumé is important. Next, I review the do's and don'ts of résumé writing and establish ground rules for what to write and what to omit. Finally, I provide examples of good résumé content that will open opportunities and poor résumé content that will close those opportunities.

Understanding the Importance of a Résumé

The *résumé* — which details your education, training, and relevant work experience with the intent of gaining employment for a specific position — is a critical component in the first steps of the hiring process and an important component in the overall hiring process. It's the first impression a potential employer has of you, your background, and your qualifications.

Résumés are used to determine whether a candidate has the potential to perform the duties listed in the job description. If the candidate does have the potential, the résumé is used to gauge the candidate's relative position against other candidates' résumés. If the résumé is weak, isn't compelling, or otherwise doesn't show that the candidate can perform the required job duties, that résumé and candidate will be dismissed. If the résumé does show promise, that résumé and candidate may be sent forward for further consideration.

If you're getting the idea that a résumé is important, you're correct. It is important, but to really appreciate its importance, you must understand how the résumé fits in the overall hiring process.

Navigating the Hiring Process

Hiring processes within companies vary, but the overall steps are similar regardless of the company or position. In general, the formal hiring process entails the following steps:

1. **A job description for an opening is posted by the company for individuals to apply.**

   The posting is generated because of a department's decision to hire a person to perform a duty.

2. **Candidates fill out the job application and submit a résumé for the job positing.**

   Typically you submit your résumé to a human resources (HR) department. Most often the résumé and job application are submitted electronically.

3. **HR reviews the pool of submitted résumés and applications against the job-posting criteria provided by the hiring department.**

   Based on HR's interpretation of the résumés and applications, only the top percentage of résumés is submitted to the department seeking to fill a position. The remaining candidates' résumés are either discarded or kept only if the top-rated candidates are not hired.

4. **The department attempting to fill the position reviews the résumés provided by HR and determines (based on the résumés) which candidates to schedule interviews with.**

5. **Members of the department conduct one or more interviews with the selected candidates.**

   The interviews may be in person, via telephone, may have technical or nontechnical questions, and there may be multiple interviews and follow-up questions.

6. **The hiring department tallies the results of the interviews, qualifications derived from résumés, and any supporting documentation and test results.**

   A selecting official determines who to make the job offer to and relays that information to HR.

7. **HR contacts the selected candidate and offers that person the job.**

   Negotiations regarding compensation, benefits, and start date occur, and if successful, the candidate comes aboard.

Note that personal referrals and recommendations are not listed in the preceding process, but depending on the company, those can play an important role at any step in the process.

Here are some key points to remember:

- ✔ HR plays a key role early on in the process, determining which résumés move forward for further consideration and which ones are discarded.
- ✔ The résumé is the means to get from the initial job posting to the critical interview with the hiring department. Without a good résumé, you never get an interview opportunity.
- ✔ Hiring decisions are made based on the résumé and interview results.

Solid qualifications coupled with a good résumé and interview techniques open many opportunities to a prospective candidate. However, before any interviews can occur, the résumé must pass the initial examinations by the HR department, and that's what I discuss next.

Getting Past the Gatekeeper

HR departments receive a stack of résumés for any job posting, and many of the people applying simply aren't qualified. Unfortunately, the multitude of unqualified applicants makes it difficult for the HR department to determine which résumés are worthy of forwarding for further consideration and which should be discarded. In many cases, the job posting is technical, and the HR team won't inherently understand what they're looking for in a qualified résumé. Getting past the HR gatekeeper is a necessary step that requires some specific résumé characteristics.

Using keywords

HR staff will be looking for specific keywords and terms provided by the department seeking to hire a candidate.

Don't expect the HR department to think outside those terms provided by the hiring department.

For example, if the hiring department is looking for an Oracle database administrator (DBA) who understands the Structured Query Language (SQL), the résumé must list *Oracle database administrator* and *SQL.* Related terms such as *DBA, sequel* (the English pronunciation of SQL), or *PL/SQL* (Oracle's SQL programming language) would likely *not* make it past the HR gatekeeper because those keywords are not on the list provided. This may not be "fair" or even reasonable, but it's a fact that applicants should understand.

The best course of action for candidates is to list as many relevant industry terms on their résumés as possible, and list them often. Use the language listed in the job posting to determine which terms to list on the résumé; those are the terms the HR department will be using as criteria.

Your résumé will be digitally uploaded and searched based on keywords. Make sure that a search on relevant keywords will show multiple "hits" for your résumé.

Navigating job-posting tools

Online job-posting tools that accept employment applications and résumés for upload make the hiring process faster and easier, but there are potential pitfalls you should be aware of.

First, know what documentation is required for the job positing and upload *all* of it. Many job postings have defined opening and closing dates, and if your complete submission is not uploaded by the closing date, your entire application packet may be discarded by HR.

Read the fine print of what is required for uploading, and ensure that everything gets uploaded and that it uploads completely. Many people have failed to be considered for jobs because they forgot to upload college transcripts or necessary professional certifications.

Consider keeping several versions of your résumé available — one that is visually appealing for in-person presentations and job fairs and a second copy that's loaded with keywords suited for upload to online postings. Be sure you've scanned copies of your school transcript(s), college degree(s), professional certification(s), and any awards and letters of reference.

After you've uploaded your documentation, be sure to review it as the HR and hiring department will see it. Upload tools often distort documents or images, and this is your opportunity to identify and catch those errors. If the relevant information is hard to identify, assume it will be even more difficult for HR and the hiring department. Take the opportunity to revise your documents before the final submission.

Don't underestimate the power of HR keyword searches and evaluations. I've seen multiple cases where highly qualified candidates seeking employment didn't make it through the initial HR selection criteria because the résumé didn't have enough keywords listed to impress the HR screeners. In one case, a candidate was attempting to switch from contractor to full-time employee status, but the HR department didn't feel his résumé qualified him for the job he was already working because he didn't include enough keywords and he was too humble about his accomplishments! The HR department should accept some blame in cases like this, but so must the candidate who didn't submit a résumé tailored to the job with the keywords HR was expecting and his accomplishments highlighted.

Knowing the Do's and Don'ts for Résumés

Entire books and classes have been devoted to résumé writing, so in this section I focus on the key elements required for résumés in the technical field. Opinions on what should be in a résumé vary among experts and they evolve over time. Additionally, what is appropriate in a résumé for a recent college graduate will be different from what a midcareer or later-career established professional will include in her résumé.

Résumé writing is as much of an art as it is a science so be flexible with updating your résumé as your situation and target job change.

Following are the characteristics of successful résumés. A successful résumé

✔ **Is concise and captures the attention of the reader quickly.** Ideally a résumé is one to three pages long, and definitely no more than five pages. Place the most important information early in the résumé and make sure it stands out to the reader. If a person has to spend more than a few moments looking for key information, his interest will dwindle and he'll move on to the next résumé.

✔ **Has clearly labeled sections:**

- Objective
- Technical skills
- Work experience
- Education
- Professional certifications, awards, or relevant training

✔ **Has action-oriented statements.** Describe the work you've done. Be descriptive, but don't write lengthy paragraphs when a short sentence or two will suffice. Be sure to work keywords into these statements.

✔ **Maintains a consistent format and voice throughout the résumé.** A résumé is a living document that will be maintained across decades of a professional career, but the flow and language should be consistent throughout the document.

✔ **Has been proofed for spelling and grammatical errors.** It's shocking how many résumés are littered with spelling errors and poor grammar. These errors suggest the candidate is a poor communicator and doesn't pay attention to detail — not the kind of impression you want to make! Ensure that keywords, technical terms, and products are spelled correctly, and match the current terminology for each relevant industry. A person researching a job positing online should find the same keywords and terms listed the same way on the résumé.

Résumés that are *not* successful share these characteristics:

✔ **Too long:** You don't want to overwhelm the reader with lengthy text descriptions that really don't provide much information. This problem is common in work experience sections. If the reader has to dig into a résumé and struggles to identify your qualifications, your résumé will likely be discarded.

✔ **Bland descriptions of work experience that don't really communicate much:** If the reader can't quickly determine what qualifications you have, the reader will become bored or frustrated and move on to another résumé.

✔ **Unexplained gaps and conflicting dates in employment, or even unexplained overlap between companies:** Résumé readers want to chart your professional career. If there is confusion about when and where you worked, the credibility of your résumé may be questioned.

✔ **Omission or minimal coverage of important information such as education, training, certifications, and awards, and too much coverage of less-critical information such as hobbies and interests:** If you're fresh out of school and you lack work experience, including club and organization membership and hobbies is reasonable, but those areas should not overshadow your education.

✔ **Sloppy format, poor grammar, inconsistent or incorrect spelling of industry terms, or spelling errors:** Errors such as these suggest that you're careless in your preparation of professional documents or, at a minimum, a poor communicator. Even if grammar and spelling errors are accepted in emails and texts, employers still expect professional documents such as résumés to be correct.

Preferences in résumés differ across industries and evolve over time, but if you follow the suggestions in this section, your résumé will always be relevant and professional.

Crafting the Right Résumé for the Position

Résumés are living documents that, once written, should be kept updated as work experience, education, and skills evolve. Many people maintain a baseline version of their résumé and create specific versions of the résumé for different job positions. This practice allows them to keep a résumé ready for short-notice, high-urgency opportunities that sometimes arise, but also have more focused résumés for targeted positions.

You may have multiple different positions you're qualified for; in this case, you'll want to maintain résumés specific for those positions. For example, if you have skills both in software development and computer system administration, you'll have two versions of the same base résumé. In one version, your software development skills are emphasized, and in the other version your system administration skills are featured.

How do you tailor a résumé for a position? Some information — such as education — will remain constant across résumés, but the following sections of the résumé should be customized:

- **Objective:** This section at the top of the résumé is where you list the position you're seeking. Use concise, focused language to state exactly what type of position you're looking for.

- **Technical skills:** Many people have multiple skills; especially in the technical field, listing these skills can become overwhelming. Position the most relevant skills at the top of this section, and possibly omit skills that aren't relevant. The idea is to quickly show the person reading the résumé that you have the skills necessary for the job, not to overload her with a glossary of technical terms.

- **Work experience:** Place additional emphasis on the specific work you've performed that is relevant to the position you're seeking. List the specific duties you've performed that will help you get the new position higher up in this section rather than at the end. Provide more descriptive narratives of how you performed that work so it's clear and obvious to the résumé reader. Using a strong, active voice that clearly shows you working in the area for the position you're seeking is critical.

Crafting a résumé for a specific position isn't difficult, and the more information you have about a position, the more you can customize a résumé for that position. If you're serious enough about a job posting that you're applying for it, then be serious enough to create a résumé that will more likely get you that position.

You aren't looking for a "job"; you're looking for a position, opportunity, or career. If you tell a prospective employer you only want a "job," ask yourself if that makes you sound more or less dedicated to the position? People perceive jobs as lowly positions you do just to make money to pay the bills, but a position, opportunity, or career denotes a higher calling requiring a greater degree of professionalism and commitment. When corresponding with prospective employers for professional positions, refrain from calling them "jobs," and focus on nobler motives — you're "seeking a position or career" or wanting "to take advantage of an opportunity." Yes, many people use the term *job* generically, but *job* is a relatively weak word and should be avoided in formal discussions.

Reviewing Sample Résumé Sections

"A picture is worth a thousand words" is a common cliché, but it's true. In this section, I walk you through parts of a sample résumé to highlight what the candidate did very well and what can be improved. I focus on several areas that people commonly have difficulty writing.

Objective

This is where you list what position you're seeking. Here are a couple examples:

> **Example 1:** Secure a senior-level application development position utilizing the Java programming language.

The first example is good. It states exactly what the candidate is looking for and leverages keywords.

> **Example 2:** Find a job that will allow me to use my IT degree to its maximum potential.

The second example is weak. It's extremely vague in terms of what position the applicant is seeking and refers to the position as a "job."

Technical skills

This section is where you list the skills that are relevant to the position you're seeking. It's an ideal place to work in keywords that the HR department (or the software they use to scan your résumé) will be looking for. Here are a couple examples:

> **Example 1:** Languages: SQL, PL/SQL, Unix Korn Shell Scripting, Java, COBOL, HTML

The first example is good. It lists specific, well-known languages and leverages keywords.

> **Example 2:** Languages: sequel, plsql, Unix shell scripting, Java, cobol/ mainframe, Html

The second example is weak. It has similar core content to the first example, but it doesn't use industry-standard names and punctuation and it's vague; the words chosen here may not show up in a keyword search.

Work experience

Your work experience should be ordered chronologically, starting with the most recent.

> **Example 1:** Acme Inc., San Francisco CA 1/2008–12/2009

This example is good. It states a specific company, location, and timeframe.

> **Example 2:** Performed as Java application developer using Java 5 and Tomcat application server version 6, and NetBeans IDE.

This example is good. It describes the work performed and the technical environment, which is important given the employment objective sought. It also takes advantage of keywords.

> **Example 3:** Led a small development team to support a new Internet banking startup company and supported complete development, test, and production deployment lifecycle.

This example is good. It defines the type of work performed, the environment, and level of expertise, which supports the employment objective of a senior-level position.

Example 4: BigTech Inc, Orlando, FL 9/2008–9/2010

This example is weak. It conflicts with the employment timeframe and location of the previous position at Acme Inc. It would require explaining because it appears at worst suspicious and at best sloppy.

Example 5: Did programming work with web applications.

This example is weak. It vaguely describes the work but doesn't provide any details and fails to list specific technologies.

Example 6: Worked on a programming team to support a web company; developed a lot of code and put it into production for XYZ system.

This example is weak. It doesn't describe the type of work performed on the development team in detail. Plus, it lists a system name that has no meaning to outsiders; a more descriptive name would've been a better choice.

Education

This is where you list the schools you attended, the dates of your enrollment (or the year you graduated), the degree you received, and any other relevant information.

Example 1

Purdue University, 1999

Baccalaureate in Computer Information Technology

GPA: 3.71/4.00

Related coursework: Oracle DBA 7.3, PL/SQL, Java

This example is good. It lists a school, date, and specific degree. Related coursework provides an opportunity to list keywords.

Only list your GPA if it was good. In this case, a 3.71 GPA is excellent so it's worth including on the résumé.

Example 2

Purdue University

Studied MIS GPA: 2.05/4.00

Related coursework: English, Chem-101, Accounting, MIS classes

Résumé ethics

There is a great amount of pressure to write a great résumé and meet all the criteria requested on a job posting; after all, careers are important and people want the best positions possible. However, do not — under any circumstances — lie, exaggerate, or otherwise misrepresent your education, training, certifications, or work experience. Most companies have a policy of immediate termination if they find out that you lied on a résumé, even if you're found out years later after successful employment. A person who lies on a résumé can't be trusted not to lie in other areas.

Most people won't outright lie, but some people may try to embellish or exaggerate. In one case, I was interviewing a person who couldn't answer basic technical questions for actions he claimed on his résumé. When I challenged the candidate on why he didn't know the information, he said, "Well, it was my team that did that technical work; I didn't actually do it myself." Needless to say, the interview ended shortly after, and the person was not hired.

This example is weak. It lists a school, but is cryptic about whether a degree was awarded, and if so, when it was awarded. The GPA is low, so it shouldn't have been included. Related coursework should focus on classes relevant to the position sought — not a general listing of classes every student would take (like English).

Chapter 14

Preparing to Nail Your Interview

*J*ob interviews combine the fear of public speaking, test-taking with an audience, and being judged by others — all while feeling as if the outcome will determine your career success or failure. To say that an interview can be stressful is an understatement! Many educated, well-qualified candidates come apart during the interview process, and many others feel a great deal of stress even if they perform well.

Although every interview is at least a little stressful, the key is to maintain perspective — no interview will make or break your entire future. Preparing can reduce your stress and improve the results you see.

In this chapter, I examine the purpose of the job interview and what employers are trying to get out of it. I fill you in on the types of interviews and how to prepare for them. More important, I explain what *you* should get out of the interview and how to market yourself at the functional and professional levels. Equipped with this information, you'll be prepared for the interview and be able to perform to your maximum potential to achieve the job you're seeking.

Dress to impress

Does it matter how you're dressed when you come in for your interview? You know the answer is yes. As much as you'd like to think that you'll be judged by your sparking personality and clever answers, you know your appearance will count. This means that even though you may work at home in your most comfortable clothes, wearing them to an interview is not advisable.

There are ways to determine what's appropriate:

✔ **Know the company.** Does it have a very serious atmosphere? Can you speak to someone who works there and find out what's acceptable?

✔ **Find out the title of the person you'll meet.** Is she a CEO, vice president, or other high-level employee? If so, wearing a suit and tie for men and a professional suit (pants or dress) for a woman is best.

✔ **Consider the job you're applying for.** Are you applying for a management job that involves supervising others? Again, professional dress is probably the right choice. Dress for the job you want, not the job you have.

Understanding Why Interviews Are Important

The interview is the focal point of any hiring process. The popular image displays it as a tense showdown where the hopeful candidate pleads his story to the skeptical panel of interviewers who ask tough questions, but are ultimately won over to the candidate's side and offer him the position.

That sometimes happens in real life, but more often, the scene is less dramatic. In reality, a good interview performs the following functions:

✔ Allows the interviewers to associate a person with the résumé and to form an impression of the candidate.

✔ Provides the interviewers an opportunity to ask questions of the candidate and judge the responses.

✔ Gives the candidate an impression of the company via the interviewers and their questions.

✔ Provides the candidate an opportunity to see if this is the company and position he really wants.

✔ Provides the company and person with an opportunity to see if there is a culture fit for each party.

✔ Provides the candidate an opportunity to ask questions of the interviewers to gain additional information not provided in the job posting.

Essentially, interviews provide both parties — interviewer and candidate — an opportunity to ask questions, exchange information, and form impressions of each other. A great deal of information is exchanged, and impressions are formed during interviews. In the following sections, I give you the tools you need to make the most of the interview.

Identifying what interviewers want to hear

Interviewers want to determine if you can functionally perform the duties of the position and if you have the personal skills to fit well in the environment and culture. At the functional level, interviewers want assurance that if they hire you, you'll be able to do what the position requires. From a personal skills perspective, interviewers want to determine if you'll fit well in the work environment or if you'll cause conflict and turbulence.

When you're interviewing for a job, make sure to do the following:

- **Reaffirm how what is on your résumé qualifies you to perform the duties of the position.** Citing examples of work experience and training are powerful tools.

- **Display your professional side of communication skills, teamwork, and commitment.** Employers don't want to hire someone they suspect will become a problem employee.

  It generally costs about $150,000 to $200,000 to fire a person, so companies want to make sure they're making the right choice.

- **Discuss how you'll serve in the position to bring improvement and business value to the company.** These messages resonate well with professional positions and show your initiative and commitment to make a positive impact on the company.

- **Showcase your most notable achievements and challenges you have overcome to display your work ethic and commitment.** Employers want to hire people who are problem solvers, so this is an opportunity to bring your successes to their attention.

- **Explain why you want the position, and display the nobler motives of seeking professional development and career growth instead of focusing only on monetary gain and amassing power, titles, and so on.**

Here are some examples of what *not* to do during an interview:

- **Speak poorly about previous and current coworkers or employers.** It's okay to indicate that you aren't satisfied in your present position, but complaining about every boss you've ever had suggests that perhaps *you* are the problem and not the boss.

✔ **Avoid revealing confidential information.** During the interview never divulge details about what your current company is doing that is not in the public domain.

✔ **Lie or misrepresent your skills, work history, training, or education.** If you don't have experience in an area, state that when asked, but talk about how you'll work to learn new skills and procedures or fix a shortcoming. It's okay to not know everything — just be sure you can describe a plan to learn the skills you need.

✔ **Display hostile, contrary, disrespectful, or otherwise unprofessional behavior during the interview or when describing your previous experiences.** You may be functionally qualified for a job, but if the interviewers believe you're going to bring turmoil to the workplace, they'll hire someone else.

✔ **Delve into irrelevant personal issues, problems, conflicts, or excuses about why you haven't succeeded in the past or why you're looking for a new position.** Check your relevant employment laws regarding disclosure of personal information. Generally, interviewers cannot ask personal questions to disqualify a person, but if you volunteer negative information, they may consider that (even unintentionally) during the selection process.

Knowing the types of interviews and tips for each

The hiring process may have zero, one, or multiple interviews depending on the position, company policies, and staffing availability of the interviewers. Hiring practices vary between and even within companies, but following are the most common forms of interviews you'll encounter.

Technical versus nontechnical

A technical interview is based on specific, technical questions, and may involve scenario-based problems for you to solve or include hands-on exercises. A technical interview is used to determine if you can functionally perform the tasks of the position, and it may serve as a way to validate your ability to perform the tasks you claim to have in your résumé. You must be able to dive deep on all technical aspects of projects listed in your résumé and be able to answer deep technical questions if you claim to be an expert on a specific technology.

A nontechnical interview is a high-level, often introductory conversation to allow the interviewers and candidate to get to know each other, exchange information, and form impressions. These interviews are often lower stress, but you should still focus on clear communications and presenting yourself in a professional manner.

The hiring process will likely involve at least one nontechnical interview, and it may or may not include a technical interview. A common technique is to include both elements in an interview, starting with nontechnical portions followed by a technical question-and-answer session.

Panel versus individual

Panel interviews include a group of interviewers asking questions, typically with one person acting as the leader or facilitator. These interviews can be intimidating for the candidate, but they allow a team of interviewers to ask questions across different areas and form impressions. Each interviewer provides input for the selection process.

Individual or one-on-one interviews involve the candidate meeting with only one interviewer. Obviously the impression you make on that single interviewer is critical. If there is a personality conflict, the impact could be negative for you.

Phone versus in-person

Phone interviews are increasingly becoming the norm, at least for initial interviews. Nonverbal communication techniques are not a factor, so focus on speaking clearly when responding to questions. Make sure you're in a quiet location with a good, static-free phone connection during a phone interview.

In-person interviews are more traditional and increasingly may not occur at all or may occur later in the interview process. Use both verbal and nonverbal communication techniques when you interview in person. Professional attire and punctuality for the meeting are also factors that influence the interviewers, so be prepared.

Studies show a great deal of communication is nonverbal: body language, posture, hand gestures, eye contact, and intonation of the words you use. Also, don't cross your arms defensively, don't play with paper or the phone, and always make eye contact. In many cases, nonverbal communication is more important than verbal. If the concept of nonverbal communication is new to you, consider studying nonverbal commination in greater detail because it's important to the relationships you form with coworkers.

Preparing for the Interview

Interviews *are* a big deal when trying to land a new position, but they don't require superhuman skills, nor should they be a source of undue stress. Like most activities, a reasonable amount of preparation will increase your effectiveness and reduce stress for the big event.

How to prepare and what to study

Being ready for an interview sends a clear signal to potential employers that you're serious about the position and you're a professional. Few things will get you rejected faster than an obvious lack of preparation or an obvious "I don't really care" attitude. Preparation for the interview generally involves the following:

✔ **Understanding the nature and requirements of the position:** Be sure you've reviewed the job posting details so you understand what the duties entail, education and certifications required, any travel and relocation requirements, and position status (contract, temporary, full-time employee, and so on).

For technical positions, be prepared for a white-boarding session. These are getting more and more popular. Practice white-boarding big data architects or spot solutions.

✔ **Nature and history of the company or organization you may be joining and the status and direction of the overall industry:** Search the company's website for official information, but also search for news articles on recent, relevant stories. Inquire within your network about the company and what working there is like — this can generate a great deal of useful information. Finally, what is the industry direction for the company and the position you're applying for? Are you going into a new, strong, and growing area? Or is it a more tenured stable position? Or is the company potentially something that may not have a great future?

Try out the company's technology. Most companies that are cloud or SaaS based allow you to try the product or service for free. So actually use the product of services. For example, for Amazon Web Services or a company that uses AWS, start up an EMR Redshift or Redshift cluster and load some data.

✔ **How your previous work experience, education, training, personality, work habits, and lifestyle make you either a good fit or perhaps not a good fit for this position:** This is perhaps the most important area to study: How do you fit well into this position? Come to the interview with facts and examples you can describe to show how and why this is a good fit for you.

✔ **Administrative details of the interview and position:** This entails the who, what, when, and why for the interview and the relative position of the interview in the overall hiring process. You want to make sure you're on time for the interview, you've met the overall hiring criteria (so far), and you're ready for the next steps in the process.

Go on some practice interviews. Interviewing itself is a skill. Practice makes perfect. Interview with a couple companies (or for a couple positions) that you aren't really interested in. If you're new to the working world or you haven't interviewed in a few years, this is important.

Preparing for the interview falls under the realm of *due diligence.* Professionals who are serious about the position will prepare, and that preparation will be recognized by the interviewers. Those who don't adequately prepare will likely end up wasting the time of everyone involved.

Be on time to the interview and ready to focus on the interview itself. Not knowing where the interview is conducted and being late, calling on a cellphone in a noisy environment, or otherwise showing that the interview is not your primary focus will at best set a disorganized or confused tone and at worst signal that you don't care about your future or the interviewers' time. Whether that is "fair" or not is irrelevant — it's a question of perception, and perception shapes hiring decisions.

Knowing what questions to ask the interviewers

Good interviews have questions going *both* ways, not just from the interviewer to interviewee. *Remember:* The interview isn't just a chance for the interviewers to determine if they want to hire you — it's also an opportunity for you to determine if this is the company you want to work for. Selecting the company you work for is a big decision, and the responsibility is on you to determine if this company is a good fit for your needs based on total compensation, the work itself, the opportunity for growth, the organizational culture and mission, and work-life balance.

Just as the interviewers have prepared questions and follow-up questions for you to answer, you should prepare questions for your potential employer. You should already know what values are important to you and what you want out of this position; use your questions to confirm if the employer meets those requirements. You should also have conducted some research on your prospective employer, and that will likely generate more questions. Your list of questions may include the following:

✔ **"What is a typical day like for the person holding this position?"** Much of this information should be captured in the job posting, but often the key information is obtained by those you'll be working with if they're conducting the interview.

✔ **"How will I be measured?"** It's important to know what their expectations for you are. You want to gear your performance to these success measures.

✔ **"What are the greatest challenges in this position?"** This is where you glean information about the work environment you may be entering.

✔ **"Describe the growth potential of this position and how it may change in five years."** This question helps determine if it is a "dead-end" job or if it has growth potential.

✔ **"Describe work-life balance in this position and company."** It is important to have accurate expectations regarding the hours worked, weekend and evening responsibilities, vacation, travel, working from home, and so on before you commit to a new position.

✔ **"Who will I be working with, and are they part of the interview process?"** This may provide a glimpse of your potential coworkers and boss. While you're forming opinions of them, they're doing the same with you.

Ask intelligent questions to gain information and show you care enough about the potential opportunity to do some preparatory research. Asking a question about what a well-known company does when the information is easily obtainable doesn't reflect well upon you. However, asking about the challenges of the company given recent industry or market shifts shows that you've done your homework and you're thinking seriously about the position.

Should you ask a potentially sensitive question if your potential employer has been in the news for something negative? For example, if the company has announced job cuts, or has been accused of an illegal or unethical behavior, or has a reputation of being a difficult place to work, do you probe into these areas? The answer is, probably yes, but be very careful about how you do it:

✔ **Consider whether the news is relevant to you and your position.** Asking about announced job cuts is relevant because it impacts your job security. However, an affair scandal involving the company's founder probably isn't relevant to your position.

✔ **Understand that the interviewer may not have all the answers or be at liberty to discuss sensitive material.** Don't be surprised if you get an incomplete answer.

✔ **If you ask the question, do so in a professional, respectful manner.** Performing research on an employer and asking a relevant, sensitive question does reflect well on you, but it can backfire if you come off as overly negative or judgmental.

Telling Your Story

By the time you've gotten to the interview, the interviewers have at least skimmed your résumé. They generally know your background and what you say you've done, but it's likely a blur among several other résumés. Your task is to become the voice (and face, if in person) of the résumé to bring it to life for the interviewers. Résumés are necessary to get an interview, but most likely how you respond during the interview determines whether you get the position. Your ability to tell your professional story and articulate how you'll perform the duties of the position in a skillful, effective, and professional manner based on your previous experience is what's most important.

Describing your professional journey

A dirty little secret in interviewing is that while the interviewers have likely skimmed over your résumé, they really haven't studied it. Most likely, they've read it quickly for education, past work experience, and keywords, but that's the extent of their review. At the extreme end, they just read your résumé ten minutes before the interview while getting coffee during an otherwise busy morning.

Don't be discouraged — it isn't personal. But it means that you have to sell yourself for the position instead of using the résumé to sell you. This is a great opportunity to talk about yourself with someone who is familiar with you but doesn't know you in detail!

Guide the interviewers down your professional path so they get to know you as a person, but also so they see how you've professionally grown into the position you are in today. Describe your education, but more important, describe your professional growth in the positions you've held. Don't reread the résumé line by line to the interviewers; instead, talk about what you've done before and how it prepares you for the position you're seeking. The goal of this (brief) discussion is to paint a picture of how you've grown professionally into the person you are now and how that makes you a good fit for the position.

Don't forget to mention key successes, major awards, and publications. Let them know that others have found your work worth recognizing.

Showing why you're a good fit

Being a good fit for the position is critical, yet so many people miss the point. It isn't enough to be a brilliant technical mind if you have to manage people and can't effectively communicate. By the same token, you can be an excellent salesperson, but if you're also required to design technical components, you need strong engineering skills. The key is to describe how and why (backed up with examples) you'll be the best person possible for the duties of the position.

Use examples in your past, including transferable skills, to show that you can step into the new position and quickly bring business value. You must impress upon the interviewers that

---

Security and your past

Increasingly, many positions require security clearances, criminal background checks, and credit checks. In some cases, background investigators may contact your references, neighbors, and even family members. This experience can be nerve-wracking, but here are some tips to help you get through this process:

✔ **Don't lie or try to cover up items that may not look good.** Employers are often forgiving and understanding if people have credit issues or even some legal or civil issues in the past, but if you're evasive about something, your evasiveness will generate a perception that you have something to hide and aren't trustworthy. This is not to say you volunteer information not requested (for example, driving 40 mph in a 35 mph zone), but if you know you have documented legal or credit issues, then upfront honesty is the best policy. Many sensitive positions in government agencies require credit checks in addition to normal criminal background checks because of the concern that a person in deep financial distress will be more susceptible to espionage offers.

✔ **Be prepared to show documentation about how any issues in the past were resolved**

and you are moving forward. In particular, credit issues and bankruptcies are a common issue for many good people, and if you can document how you took corrective actions and are moving forward, that can alleviate many employers' concerns.

✔ **Prepare your references and neighbors that they may be contacted for an interview.** Being cold-called by an investigator and asked questions about someone looking for a job is unsettling. Help yourself by letting your references know they may be contacted for an interview.

✔ **Expect security reviews to take a long time, require a great deal of documentation, and be frustrating.** Many people become discouraged and withdraw from the hiring process when they otherwise would've passed if they were just a little more patient and willing to work with investigators.

Many great positions require background investigators to be hired and, once hired, to remain in that position. Take good care of yourself and your reputation so that you can take advantage of these opportunities.

✔ You have the quantitative skills to perform the duties of the position at a very high level (in other words, you can do the job).

✔ You have the *hard skills* (ones that can be taught and measured) and *soft skills* (ones that have to do with personality, like getting along with people) to perform the duties of the position. Specifically, you can get along with your coworkers and management chain effectively and not be a problem employee.

✔ You *want* and will value the position; it's not a stepping stone, and you'll give your full energies to being successful.

Many good people are naturally humble and refrain from selling themselves during an interview. That's a shame because these people lose out on great positions and promotions. ***Remember:*** It's okay to talk about your hard-earned accomplishments and relate how they provide business value during your interview process. No one can promote yourself as well as you can, so during the interview you must be an advocate for yourself and what you can provide for the prospective employer!

Employers don't want to hire toxic people in their organizations if they can avoid it. During your interview, give your interviewers every reason to believe that you'll get along well with other coworkers in an appropriate, professional manner. More important, after you're hired, make sure you do get along with other employees in a supportive, professional manner! Research and real-world experience show that productivity and job satisfaction are increased when people work well together; team unity and getting along with others benefits both the company and the people involved. Interviewers know this and will make their selections accordingly.

Unlocking Success in a Behavioral Interview

A common form of interview is the *behavioral interview*. In a behavioral interview, you're asked about situations you experienced previously and how you resolved the situation. Unlike a standard interview, where you have to explain what you *would* do in a given theoretical situation or answer a question about yourself, a behavioral interview is based on what you have done *in the past* and why.

Examples of behavioral interview questions include the following:

✔ Describe a situation you faced where you had multiple projects with limited resources and timelines. How did you manage the workload?

✔ Have you ever faced a personality conflict with a coworker and how did you respond?

✔ Describe a situation where you were faced with a difficult or stressful decision and how you made and implemented your decision.

Behavioral interviews are designed to give employers a chance to see how you've responded to situations in the past with the assumption that your past actions will determine how you'll respond in the future.

Getting ready for probing questions

Interviewers will ask *probing* questions to find out why you took the action you did, what factors you considered, what (if anything) you would do differently, and if so, why. There may not be a "wrong" answer, but there certainly are better answers than others.

Here are some examples of probing questions:

✔ Do you operate within professional norms and include your management chain and team when appropriate? If not, why not, and was that the best course of action in that situation?

✔ Are you a self-starter with initiative, or do you rely more on a structured environment and a more dictatorial hierarchy?

✔ Were you able to accomplish your mission amid a climate of bickering and petty politics? If not, was there a valid reason why not and how did you recover?

Expect your responses to generate follow-up questions and comments from your interviewers — that's natural. If you can explain *why* you performed a certain way, your logic and problem solving will be what interviewers positively remember even if they may not have taken the same course of action themselves.

Turning probing questions into opportunities

When responding to a probing question about a situation you wish you had handled more effectively, did you openly admit your mistake and discuss how you learned from it? There is nothing wrong with admitting a mistake or something you could have done better; in fact, that trait shows professionalism, maturity, and honesty. Unless you grossly acted unprofessionally or illegally in a situation you're describing, the interviewers are more focused on your logic and reasoning than the specific outcome.

Use probing questions as a way to tell more of your story, show yourself as both a real person and as a dedicated professional, and underscore how you work with the company's best interests in mind. This is an opportunity to showcase the best qualities you have, your growth potential, and how you can serve as an asset to the potential employer.

Feel free to inquire if a scenario you're being asked about is common in the position you're seeking. For example, if you notice a series of questions about how you work in chaotic environments or under tight timelines with few resources, you would be justified in asking if that's the environment you're entering. Interviewers often ask questions that reflect their current work environment and challenges; you can use that to glean more information about the position.

Telling war stories

An interview is a great opportunity to tell relevant war stories about situations you have experienced and how you handled them correctly or learned from them. War stories are similar to experiences related in behavioral interviews, but they're experiences you've selected in advance — not experiences selected by the interviewer. War stories show interviewers that you have real experience.

To be most effective, a good war story should

✔ Be relevant to the position you're pursuing, or at least have some transferable learning points if it happened outside the office.

✔ Be brief and have one or two easily identified key points.

✔ Not be overly negative or be used to attack a former employer, current employer, or coworkers. You don't want to come off as a complainer or vengeful. Also, not using real names (company, client, or individual) is the way to go, unless real names are absolutely essential for the story.

✔ Show how you faced a real situation and what you did to solve it or how you learned a lesson from it.

✔ Have an element of humor if possible. People love good stories and are drawn to people who can spin a good tale. Giving your interviewers a good laugh makes you far more memorable in a good way than someone devoid of personality or humor.

Concerned you don't have any good stories? You shouldn't be. Odds are, if you have any work experience or even project group experience in school, you were exposed to some event where a challenge occurred, you responded to that challenge and either you were successful or you learned a lesson from that experience.

Have you ever said something but it came out wrong or had the exact opposite effect you intended? Don't worry — that happens to everyone and as the stress builds (such as during an interview) so does the likelihood of making that mistake. If you say something silly; the best response is to fix it with a follow-up explanation or correction with humility and confidence. Interviewers know interviewees are under pressure and will respect the person who responds with, "I didn't explain myself clearly on that point — let me rephrase it" instead of trying to defend a poor response.

Unlocking the Key Aspects to a Good Case Interview

Another common form of interview is the *case interview.* In a case interview, you're given a specific problem or scenario that you must solve during the interview. Instead of recounting how you solved a problem in the past, or how you might solve a problem in the future, you're expected to solve a given problem in the interview.

Here are some examples of case interview questions:

- ✔ You have a new team of employees that must provide operational support for the help desk. The previous team was a contracting firm that was terminated because of poor performance. How do you proceed?

- ✔ You're in charge of the budget for a large IT services hosting company. Your technical folks are requesting new hardware for an aging infrastructure, but their request exceeds your budget. How do you support your technical folks while maintaining your budget?

Case interviews are designed to give employers a chance to see how you solve problems based on scenarios defined by the interviewers. Interviewers are less concerned about your final answer; they want to understand how you think and solve problems.

Structuring problems

During the case interview, you're likely permitted to ask questions to gain more information about the scenario. This is intended to determine how you identify the core problems amid a wide description of symptoms. Asking good questions and identifying the core problem(s) is critical in the real work environment, so be sure to ask similar questions during the interview. The important takeaway is to understand that the scenario may have different layers to it that you must uncover as you identify the problem.

Exhibiting analytics and reasoning skills

The nature of the position and the type of scenario will influence the analytical and reasoning skills you use; be sure to match the right methods to the given situation. For example, if you're working with a people issue, your soft skills are most helpful. Conversely, if you're working on a finance or engineering problem, you need to use your hard skills to solve the problem.

The interviewers will be interested in the logic and methods you use to solve the problem more than they'll care about the final answer, so be able to justify your decision making as you go. Even if you select the "wrong" method, if you can still logically articulate why you did so, you'll gain partial credit and the respect of the interviewers.

Showcasing business skills and industry awareness

Displaying excellent awareness of the industry, market trends, and the required business skills makes you a much more attractive candidate than someone who only knows the raw technical aspects of the position. Leaders can articulate the direction of their industry and describe their actions in terms of business value, which managers easily understand. These are skills many people lack and are an opportunity for you to stand out over your competition.

As you work through the case interview (or even a behavioral interview), take care to speak in terms of showing the business value of your actions and how they're in line with the direction of your industry.

Displaying good presentation skills

Poor presentation skills, apparent lack of confidence, or obvious disorganization have prevented many people from achieving their maximum potential. Especially during an interview, be sure to communicate clearly as you articulate your answers to questions.

Consider these factors when presenting and communicating during an interview:

- ✔ **Slow down, organize your thoughts into a few key points, and then present them in a relaxed manner to your interviewers.** Interviewers will have more respect for a well-reasoned argument than stream-of-consciousness responses blurted out in a hurried, unfocused manner.

✔ **Don't be afraid to ask for clarity.** You can ask the interviewer to repeat or rephrase the question if you don't understand it. It's better to ask then to answer a question he didn't ask.

✔ **Emphasize the logic behind your decisions and how they're supportive of business value for the company.** If you can show how you applied logic and why it was geared to benefit the company, it's difficult for the interviewers to not see you in a positive light.

✔ **Consider using a whiteboard if possible to add a visual element to your presentation.** For example, if you whiteboard an architectural diagram of a computer system you managed as you talk about how you designed that system in your last job, you're showing that you know the technical side but can present to an audience; this is a double-win for you.

Only do this if you've presented with a whiteboard before and you're totally comfortable with it — you don't want your first time through to be in a job interview!

✔ **Don't be afraid of questions.** In fact you should encourage questions and dialog with your interviewers. This is your chance to take control and show your initiative and confidence. Don't be afraid to seize the opportunity!

Many people are afraid of public speaking, but verbal communication is important — even in this age of emails and text messages. You don't have to be a professional speaker, but if you can't get your points across, you should consider working on this skill outside the interview process. Many classes and public speaking clubs are available — they can be a way of turning a weakness into a strength.

Showing Motivation and Excitement

Put yourself in the shoes of the interviewers. Given two roughly equal candidates, would you hire the person with energy and enthusiasm, or would you hire the unmotivated and uninspired "dud"? Taken even further, interviewers are more likely to "take a chance" on a less-qualified candidate if that person is eager to learn and clearly will commit himself to the new company and position.

Don't be afraid to mention something you're passionate about — reading, writing, a hobby. It demonstrates that you have a curiosity for things.

Despite the weight that résumés, work experience, education, and certifications carry, showing motivation and energy to want a position during the interview process is a key advantage. In this section, I show you how to capitalize on this advantage.

Displaying your initiative

Performing research on the company, its industry, and potential challenges displays that you care enough about the position to do your homework on it. Take action to show the potential employer that you've already considered the requirements of the position and you're prepared to meet those requirements.

One example of displaying initiative is how you've prepared to obtain any technical or professional certifications required by the position. Many jobs require certifications or specific skillsets. When you can show that you've already obtained those certifications or skillsets (or at least have a plan to obtain them), it's a clear indicator that you're serious about the position.

Making it easy to hire you

Employers want to quickly hire people who are ready to work and won't cause problems once they're past the probationary period for the company. Having any necessary technical or professional certifications is a great start, but attitude and presentation are important, too. For example

- ✔ **Indicate when you could start for the company, if hired.** As a courtesy, give you current employer two weeks' notice. If you don't, your future employer will question your integrity and professionalism.

  Note: Two weeks' notice is standard in the United States, but if you live in a place where that time period is traditionally longer, it's important to follow the norm in your area.

- ✔ **Don't badmouth your current employer or coworkers.** If you do, the interviewers will wonder if you'll be talking negatively about them next.

- ✔ **Be upfront about any special considerations.** If you have any special circumstances that would impact coming to the new employer such as having to move a great distance or nondisclosure agreements (NDAs), mention them now, but also identify your solutions. This tells the interviewers that you're upfront and honest, but you also have solutions to any issues.

- ✔ **Be upbeat, pleasant, and professional in all your interactions with the interviewers and their staff.** Be nice to everyone you deal with, not just the interviewers you speak with directly. Don't give anyone a reason to question your professionalism, integrity, or motivations.

Simply following good citizenship rules you learned as a kid is a good start. It's amazing how many people sabotage themselves out of good employment opportunities.

Telling them you want this position

Stating that you would want this position does *not* make you look desperate; it makes you look *confident*. Of course, the context of how you state you want the job is the key. Here's an example of the wrong way versus the right way to state you want the job.

> **Wrong way:** "Since I was fired from my last job, I've had a tough time finding anything else. I really need this to pay my mortgage."

This denotes desperation and commitment to a paycheck (just a job) rather than commitment to the position (a career). At best, if you're hired, you'll likely be offered a lower salary because you're perceived as desperate.

> **Right way:** "I've taken some time to evaluate where I want to go next with my career. This position is a great fit for what I want to do next with my life, and I'd like to the opportunity to show you what I can do."

This indicates that you're thoughtful about your professional development and you realize the position must benefit *both* you and the employer.

 Let the interviewers know that this is a position you want for purposes of professional development and personal growth and that you're excited for the opportunity. Those are the good impressions you want the interviewers to be remembering you by as they work through the selection process.

Ending on a high note

Finishing the interview isn't difficult if you've been confident, energized, and professional. Even if you didn't answer every question correctly or you had some missteps, you can still improve your chances by doing the following:

- ✔ **Respect the scheduled ending time.** Certainly answer questions and be sure to get your key questions answered, but don't drag out an interview unnecessarily.

- ✔ **Don't bring up any mistakes you made or areas where you lack skills unless you have a strong rebuttal to reframe those areas as positives.** Even then, I don't recommend it.

- ✔ **Don't ask if you have the job or apply negative pressure on the interviewers.**

✔ **Ask what the next steps are in the selection process and when you may hear more information.** The interviewers likely have more interviews to conduct, and they may not be the final selecting authority. If there are further steps or background investigations, find out what you need to do for these steps. If there are restrictions on how the company may contact you, such as not calling your current employer's office phone, let them know that information.

✔ **Recap why you want the position and why it would be beneficial to both parties that you're hired.**

✔ **Thank them for their time and the opportunity to interview with them.**

You should finish the interview by displaying your profession, confidence, and tempered eagerness for the position.

I know of a candidate who was not fully technically qualified for an entry-level position, but he flatly stated, "This is my dream job. I know I'm a little lacking on the skills, but I'm willing to study on my own time to come up to speed." His statement and enthusiasm were sincere, and he had a background that indicated he could learn the technical aspect, so the interviewers took a chance on this person. The candidate proved to be a highly valued member of the team, and it was his enthusiasm that allowed him to stand out among other candidates.

Part V
The Part of Tens

 For ten public datasets and where to find them, check out www.dummies.com/extras/gettingabigdatajob.

In this part . . .

- ✔ Find out how to maximize social media in your job hunt.
- ✔ Identify key questions you need to be able to answer for a good interview.

Chapter 15

Ten Ways to Maximize Social Media in Your Job Hunt

Your public face to the world — the version of yourself you put online — is your brand. If you manage your brand well, you're more likely to be seen and contacted by recruiters. If you have a poorly crafted online brand, the opposite is true. Once you get an interview, employers are likely to research your professional and personal social media presence.

In this chapter, I give you ten practical ways to spiff up your brand, get noticed online, and maintain that reputation as your career grows.

Google Yourself

You want to search for yourself online to see what potential employers will see when they check you out, because they likely will. What comes up (or doesn't come up) will tell you where to start your personal brand management.

When potential employers search for you, you want to be found easily and you want your accomplishments to be clear.

When you Google yourself, be sure to click the links for News, Images, and Videos. Some of those party photos, old headshots, or stupid high school videos may still be out there.

Get Rid of Unflattering Pictures

When you search for yourself online (see the preceding section), you may come across some pictures of yourself that you don't exactly want potential employers to see. You want to try to remove as many of those images as you possibly can. It's probably impossible to remove all of them. Go to the place where the image resides and delete it. This may or may not work, depending on how many places it has been shared.

Images may have been cached by Google, and it may take a while for deleted images to disappear from web searches.

Facebook, Twitter, and Instagram allow people to tag each other in photos. The good news is, you can remove yourself from photos you've been tagged in. If you have profiles on any of these sites, check to see which photos you've been tagged in and remove yourself from any photos you wouldn't want a future employer to see. (The steps for removing yourself from a photo vary from one platform to the next, so consult the Help system of the service you're using or contact Support for more information.)

Be Your Own Best Editor

If you've written a blog, posted in online forums, posted videos on YouTube, or done any other kind of writing, picture taking, or video making on the Internet, you need to identify any posts that you wouldn't want a potential employer to see.

Do a Google search not just on your name, but on any online screen names you've used over the years. Because your real name may be attached to the screen name, you want to see what the search reveals.

If you've posted to a forum, log in and find the messages that you posted and either delete or edit them. Most forums allow for editing by the author after they've been posted.

Get On Google+

If you aren't on Google+ yet, you may be thinking, "Oh, jeez, yet another social media site I have to maintain. Why bother?" But it's worth your time to set up a Google+ profile and make sure it's current. Because Google+ is a part of Google, the content you put there will be prioritized by it in any Google search.

Use LinkedIn Like a Pro

LinkedIn is the most widely used social media site to connect people for business purposes. It's used to share knowledge, create discussion groups, and find business contacts. Plus, LinkedIn is by far the most widely used social networking site for those seeking employment.

LinkedIn shows job ads that match your profile. For this reason, make sure your profile has the right keywords and content.

Follow these tips to maximize both views and quality of views on LinkedIn:

✔ **Treat your LinkedIn profile like a résumé.** Your LinkedIn profile is an online résumé, working for you 24/7. Make sure that you've carefully thought out every detail you include in your profile.

If your résumé doesn't match your LinkedIn profile, you're setting yourself up for problems. Make sure they match in every detail. You don't want to have to explain why they're different.

✔ **Highlight your achievements.** Focus on achievements that have measureable results or a specific impact on the company for which you worked. For example, you should say, "Decreased big data query time by 30 percent" instead of "Improved big data system performance." Steer clear of generalities and fuzzy job titles or duties.

✔ **Upload a good-quality headshot.** Your profile picture should be welcoming and appropriate. Pick something appropriate for the job you want. If you're a programmer, you probably don't need to be wearing a suit, but a selfie probably isn't the best idea, either. You may want to go to a professional photo studio to have your portrait taken. If you're going for a less-formal look, have a friend with a good-quality digital camera take a picture of you. And don't forget to smile!

✔ **Follow companies and industry influencers.** Following companies gives you a couple benefits:

- The firms you want to work for will post jobs, and those jobs will be highlighted for you on LinkedIn.

- You can see what companies and topics are interested in.

Don't follow too many companies, groups, or influencers. The kitchen-sink approach makes it look like you have no focus. Start with a list of ten companies you'd like to work for, and put all your focus on them.

✔ **Use multimedia.** LinkedIn allows you to post videos, slides, and links to books, articles, and blog posts. Take this opportunity to highlight your many dimensions.

✔ **Cut the fluff.** Stay away from industry buzzwords or descriptions that don't mean anything. Nothing says "fluff" like a LinkedIn profile that says you're a "leading strategic thinker who drives value for customers." This sentence not only says nothing about you but may communicate that you talk without having anything to say.

✔ **Check your settings.** LinkedIn allows you to control what you share. For example, when you update your profile with skills and experience, you can broadcast that information to your network or keep it on the down low. When you add new contacts, you can alert your network or not. Decide what you want to share and make sure your settings reflect that.

✔ **Keep it short and sweet.** Don't use ten words when five will do. For example, "Led the Southeast Region in sales for five years" is better than "Consistently was the leading sales rep in the Southeast Region for five years in a row." Hit the point and move on.

✔ **Don't blindly invite.** Make sure you have a reason, connection, and custom message for the people you try to connect with on LinkedIn. Your introduction message should provide context and value to them.

✔ **Don't oversend.** Make sure you don't update your status all the time if you're broadcasting those updates to your network. In group discussions, don't publish anything to the discussion unless it adds real value to the conversation. What and how you write says a lot about you.

✔ **Don't be creepy.** If someone visits your profile, don't reach out to him just because you saw he visited your profile. If he wants to make contact, he will.

Start Blogging

The first step in being an expert is saying "Why *not* me?" Find a topic that you're knowledgeable about, and do all you can to go deeper. Post your thinking, insights, and findings in a blog. You can easily set up a blog — check out WordPress (www.wordpress.com), Blogger (www.blogger.com), Typepad (www.typepad.com), and Tumblr (www.tumblr.com).

Plan what you're going to blog for a period of time, and make sure you regularly update your blog — you don't want a potential employer to find a blog that you haven't updated in months. You're better off posting once a week than posting once a day and running out of things to say. Never start a blog post with, "Sorry I haven't posted in a while."

Become an Expert

If you don't have time to blog, but you want to build your brand as an expert, consider frequenting Q&A websites like Stack Overflow (`www.stackoverflow.com`) and Quora (`www.quora.com`). Build your brand and reputation as someone who has knowledge and is willing to share it. Link your answers to your online profiles. When recruiters check you out online, your reputation for being knowledgeable and willing to coach others will be a boost.

Focus on Facebook

Facebook is more than just a way to connect with friends from high school or share your latest vacation pictures. It's a great tool to network for a new job. There are a few things you can do to leverage this massive network:

- **Update your profile.** Make sure you fill out your "About" section with your professional history. Recruiters will use this to find you.

- **Leverage the network.** Take time to engage your own network or ask for help. Don't be casual with your postings, but be professional. If you want to work at General Electric, let folks know that you're interested in finding a connection there, and maybe someone you're Facebook friends with will be willing to help you.

- **Connect with companies.** Follow the companies you'd like to work for. They'll post new jobs, talk about career fairs, and maybe even connect back to you.

#UseTwitter

Twitter is an excellent way to keep an eye on the companies you want to work for someday. You can also use Twitter to do a little research and find out who recruits for the firms you like. For example, if you want to work for General Electric, you can search LinkedIn for "GE, Recruiting" and find a list of recruiters. They'll often link to their Twitter accounts on their LinkedIn profiles. Follow those people on Twitter. They'll post new jobs, information about job fairs, and tips for getting hired. When you follow these folks, it lets people know you're on the market.

Check Your Klout

One of the best ways to get a measure of your impact on social media is to check your Klout score (`http://klout.com`). Klout is a site that assigns you a score from 1 to 100 based on how often you engage others on the major social platforms. The more influential you are, the higher your score. If you're just starting out, it's more likely that your score will be below 30. Klout looks at the accumulation of things like retweets on Twitter and Likes on Facebook. If no one responds to your content, your Klout score remains low.

Chapter 16

Ten Interview Questions and Answers You Need to Know

*Y*ou may have already experienced that classic interview question. You know the one I mean. The employer asks, "Tell me your greatest weakness." And you say something like, "Well, I just work too darn hard." I was once asked that question in an interview for an internal promotion at a major credit card firm. I said, "When I get angry, I throw things." It was well received, but I wouldn't recommend such a humorous approach unless I was sure that the interviewer seemed receptive.

Know the corporate culture before you interview. They're likely probing for cultural fit as much as they are for competency. There are a few things you can do to get insight into corporate culture:

✔ **Check out the company's Careers page.** It often lists the company's vision, values, and mission.

✔ **Read the About Us page.** This page often tells more than just the function of the company — it should give some insight into why and how the company was founded. These are often drivers for culture.

✔ **Read sites like Vault (www.vault.com) or Glassdoor (www.glassdoor. com), which has former and current employees post what it's like to work there.**

Read through each of the questions in this chapter and reflect on how you would respond. The corresponding answers should give you guidelines about what the interviewer is trying to find out.

Interviewers aren't just looking for the answer to the question — they're trying to understand more about you as a potential candidate. You should go into an interview thinking about the kind of candidate you're trying to be. Are you an innovator, an execution expert, or an extremely efficient programmer? Your answers should have a coherent theme.

Can You Tell Me about Yourself?

This open-ended question is sometimes used as an icebreaker. It's your opportunity to set the pace and make a good first impression.

Here are some ways *not* to respond to this question:

- ✔ **Don't say, "That's a great question" or "Thanks for asking that."** Don't start *any* answer with crutch phrases like these.

- ✔ **Don't start with your life story.** The interviewer doesn't care where you were born or how many siblings you have.

- ✔ **Don't recite your résumé.** Most people are nervous and fall back on a chronology of every job they've ever had, but the interviewer already has that information on your résumé.

Here are some strategies to employ when answering this question:

- ✔ **Start strong.** Think of a strong opening statement that establishes who you are and the value you can provide. For example, maybe you started life as a programmer, but you really saw a future in big data. You went to grad school, earned an advanced degree in analytics, and you're ready to grab that first big data job.

  A weak intro to this question would be, "Well, I started out after school as a programmer. That really didn't excite me, so I went to grad school to learn more about big data." A better way to say the same thing would be: "I love technology and the challenges they bring. I started life as a programmer but quickly realized the power of big data and knew I wanted to be a part of that. . . ."

- ✔ **Focus on the attributes and qualities you want them to know about.** If you want the company to know you're self-directed, give examples where you've succeeded without supervision. If you're great at execution, talk about a project that you turned around.

It's often helpful to limit the amount of background that you give. You don't need to go into your last five jobs in detail. Focus on the last five years.

When you talk about your history, remember that you're telling a story. Make it enjoyable and think about engaging your interviewer.

Managers appreciate the ability to relay key information quickly. Prepare several answers to this question in case you need to adjust your answer based on the situation.

What Are Your Goals?

This is the most important question — the one you *must* have an excellent answer for. If you wait too long to reply or try to make up an answer on the fly, you'll project a lack of drive, planning, and focus.

Employers want people who are results oriented. It can be a bonus if your career goals fit the mission of the company you're applying to. Avoid discussing goals that are only about you and how the job will benefit you. You want to show how you provide value to the company. False humility doesn't work here either. Cite two or three goals that are personal and professional. That will show a good balance of work and the multiple dimensions your personal life.

Here are a few example answers:

- I want to be a part of a high-growth company.
- Within three years, I'd like to help a company IPO.
- Within five years, I'd like to be leading a team of big data professionals.

Why Do You Want to Work Here?

Throughout my career, I've been in a position to hire both technical and business professionals. I've asked this question many times in interviews because it gives me a good chance to see if the candidate has done her homework and understands the mission of my organization.

Your answer to this question can quickly show that you know the business and can contribute. Connect *why* you want to work there with *how* you're going to make it successful. Make sure you're very specific. For example, if you're working for a big data product company that makes visualization software using Java and Hadoop, connect your programming ability to deliver software quickly and get to sales faster. Tie your skills to the goals of the business or department you want to work for.

Use positive phrases like *I can* and *I will* rather than hypothetical phrases like *I could* or *I would*. Focus on what you can do or have done.

Why Should We Hire You?

This answer should look a bit like the previous one. Show your knowledge of the firm and why you're the perfect fit.

Have you ever been through an interview ready to answer a specific question that shows how great you are, but you were never asked it? This question is a great one to insert the answer to the question you wished they would have asked you but didn't. In many interviews, there are a few traits, projects, or accomplishments you may not get to talk about? So, if you get asked, "Why should we hire you?", mention some of the positives that haven't come up yet. Make sure you show a real desire to work at the company.

You're essentially in business for yourself during the interview. You have a service they need, and your job is to let them know what that is and how valuable you'll be to their firm.

Why Do You Want to Leave Your Current Job?

If you currently have a job or you're new to the job market, make your answer to this question about personal and professional growth. Don't indicate that you want more money or you don't get along with your boss. This is an open-ended question that allows you to reveal positive traits about yourself.

If you don't have a job, don't worry! Stay positive, and make it a part of your story. Pivot to how you've been preparing for the next stage in life, something beyond just looking for a new position. Tell a good story!

Can You Give Me an Example of a Time When You Had to Make a Decision with Limited Information?

This question reveals a lot about how you make choices. It gives the interviewer the opportunity to probe how you frame and solve problems. This is your chance to tell how you manage the risks and benefits of your choice. Prepare an answer that illustrates your leadership as well as your ability to make the tough choice.

Whenever you get a question with "Tell me about a time . . ." or "Give me an example of . . .", be very specific about your role in the answer. Our culture promotes teamwork, so answers tend to have a lot of *we*s. Get rid of the word *we* when giving examples. It's a red flag that shows that you didn't actually have significant impact on the story you're telling. It forces a good interviewer to probe further to uncover what you actually did.

How Do Others View You?

This question gives you a chance to focus on one or two strengths about you. You should go for two good attributes that are in high demand for the role and the culture of the firm. Focus on attributes like loyalty, leadership, and dependability. Some interviewers will throw this at you in the beginning with a follow-up question asking for specific references and if your references can be contacted. This isn't mean spirited, but it is meant to see how you react so the interviewer can gauge your truthfulness and set the tone for honest answers going forward.

Can You Tell Me about a Time When You Made a Mistake?

Questions like this are not intended to reveal your weaknesses. Instead, they're designed to see how you react to problems. Are you accountable? How did you fix the problem you created? Can you tell a story that shows how you built additional trust with your client/customer/boss because of the way you handled the situation?

Most of the time, your answers need to be recent to maintain credibility, but this is an example where it's okay for the mistake to be a long time ago. This shows that even though you've made mistakes, it may have been a while ago and you've learned from them. This is actually a great time to offer a follow-up example where you were in a similar situation and *avoided* the mistake.

Can You Tell Me about Some of Your Accomplishments?

Make sure you answer this question with a very recent answer. Candidates who don't have accomplishments in the past year are suspect. Keep it professional and focus on something that can be tied to a measurable impact.

I recently interviewed a candidate who went on and on about how he led an effort for a custom offering for a customer. In the end, it meant only $200 per month in revenue.

Don't underwhelm the interviewer with your response. Do make sure you have supporting data — cost savings, time savings, added revenue, a big client landed, and so on.

Have You Ever Disagreed with Your Boss? If So, How Did You Handle It?

How you handle this question shows how you handle both conflict and differing ideas. After all, you'll be working with people, and with people, there will be conflict and competing ideas. Make sure you come up with an example for this question. Don't say you can't recall a time of conflict or when you wanted to take a different course from your boss. Instead, come up with an issue that's quite minor. Focus on the framework you used to come to a resolution. Did you respect and listen to others' ideas? Were you right and felt slighted, or did you capitulate a minor issue to build a relationship?

Chapter 17

Ten Free Data Science Tools and Applications

Data Science For Dummies,
Lillian Pierson

In This Chapter

▶ Getting creative with free R packages for data visualization

▶ Using open-source tools for scraping, collecting, and handling your data

▶ Analyzing your data with free open source tools

▶ Having fun with visualizations in other open-source applications

*V*isualizations are a vitally important part of the data scientist's toolkit. With them, you can leverage the brain's capacity to quickly absorb visual information. Because data visualizations are a very effective means of communicating data insights, many tool and application developers work hard to ensure that the platforms they design are simple enough for even beginners to use. An application that is simple enough to be useful to a beginner can sometimes be useful to more advanced data scientists, but other times data science experts simply need more technical tools to help them delve deeper into datasets.

In this chapter, I present ten free web-based applications that you can use to do more advanced data science tasks. You can download and install many of these applications on your home machine and most of the downloadable applications are available for multiple operating systems.

WARNING! Always make sure to read and understand the licensing requirements of any app you use. Protect yourself by determining how you're allowed to use the products you've created.

Making Custom Web-Based Data Visualizations with Free R Packages

The packages and tools that I introduce in this section are useful for creating really cool data visualizations, but they require you to code in R statistical programming language to be able to use them. This said, because you have to code things up yourself with these packages and tools, you can create results that are more customized for your needs.

In this section, I discuss using Shiny, rCharts, and rMaps to create really neat-looking web-based data visualizations.

Getting Shiny by RStudio

Not long ago, if you needed to do serious data analysis, you'd need to know how to use a statistics-capable programming language like R. And if you needed to make interactive web visualizations, you'd have to know how to code in languages like JavaScript or PHP. Of course, if you wanted to do both simultaneously, you'd have to know how to code in an additional two or three more programming languages. In other words, web-based data visualization based on statistical analyses was a cumbersome task.

The good news is that things have changed. Because of the work of a few dedicated developers, the walls between analysis and presentation have crumbled. With the 2012 launch of RStudio's Shiny package (http://shiny.rstudio.com), both statistical analysis and web-based data visualization can be carried out in the same framework.

RStudio — already, by far, the most popular integrated development environment (IDE) for R — developed the Shiny package to allow R users to create web apps. Web apps made in Shiny run on a web server and are *interactive* (with them, you can interact with the data visualization and do things like move sliders, check boxes, or click on the data itself). Because these apps run on a server, they're considered *live* — when you make changes to the underlying data, those changes are automatically reflected in the appearance of the data visualization. Web apps created in Shiny are also *reactive* — in other words, they output updates instantly in response to a user interaction, without the user having to click a Submit button.

If your goal is to quickly use a few lines of code to instantly generate a web-based data visualization application, you can use R's Shiny package to do this. What's more, if you want to customize your web-based data visualization app to be more aesthetically appealing, you can do that by simply editing the HTML, CSS, and JavaScript that underlie the Shiny application.

Because Shiny produces server-side web apps, you'll need a server host and you'll need to know how to host your web app on a server before you can make useful web apps using the package.

Shiny runs a public web server called ShinyApps.io (www.shinyapps.io). You can use that service to host an app there for free, or you can pay to host there if your requirements are more resource intensive.

Charting with rCharts

Although R has always been famous for its beautiful static visualizations, only recently has it been possible to use R to produce web-based interactive data visualizations.

Things changed with the advent of rCharts (www.rcharts.io). rCharts is an open-source package for R that takes your data and parameters as input, and then quickly converts those to a JavaScript code block output. Code block outputs from rCharts can use one of many popular JavaScript data visualization libraries, including NVD3, Highcharts, Richskaw, xCharts, Polychart, and Morris.

To see some examples of data visualizations created using rCharts, check out rCharts Gallery (www.rcharts.io/gallery). In this gallery, you'll see data graphics as simple as standard bar charts and scatter plots, as well as more complex data graphics like chord diagrams and hive plots.

Mapping with rMaps

rMaps (http://rmaps.github.io) is the brother of rCharts. Both of these open-source R packages were crafted by Ramnath Vaidyanathan. Using rMaps, you can create animated or interactive chloropleths, heat maps, or even maps with annotated location droplets — like those found in the JavaScript mapping libraries Leaflet, CrossLet, and Data Maps.

If your goal is to create a spatial data visualization that has interactive sliders that users can move to select the data range they want to see, then rMaps offers you a perfect solution.

If you're an R user and you're accustomed to using the simple R Markdown syntax to create web pages, you'll be happy to know that it's easy to embed both rCharts and rMaps in R Markdown.

If you prefer Python to R, Python users aren't being left out on this trend of creating interactive web-based visualizations within one platform. Python users can use server-side web app tools like Flask (a less user-friendly, but more powerful tool than Shiny) and the Bokeh and Mpld3 modules to create client-side JavaScript versions of Python visualizations. The Plot.ly tool has a Python API (as well as ones for R, MATLAB, and Julia) that you can use to create web-based interactive visualizations directly from your Python IDE or command line.

Checking Out More Scraping, Collecting, and Handling Tools

You can use web scraping to derive really interesting and unique datasets for your data-driven stories. In this section, I fill you in on the free tools that you can use to scrape data or images. These include Import.io, ImageQuilts, and DataWrangler.

Scraping data with Import.io

Have you ever tried to copy and paste a table from Wikipedia into a Microsoft Office document and then not been able to get the columns to line up correctly? Frustrating, huh? This is exactly the pain point that Import.io (pronounced "import eye oh") was designed to address.

Import.io (`https://import.io`) is a free desktop application that, with a few clicks of the mouse, you can use to painlessly copy, paste, clean, and format any part of a web page. You can even use Import.io to automatically crawl and extract data from multipage lists.

Using Import.io, you can scrape data from a simple or complicated series of web pages:

- ✔ To scrape a simple series of web pages, access them through simple hyperlinks, in Page 1, Page 2, Page 3, . . . series.
- ✔ To scrap a complicated series of web pages, fill in a form or choose from a drop-down list, and submit your scraping request to the tool.

Import.io's most impressive feature is its capability to observe a few mouse-clicks to learn what you want, and then offer you ways that it can automatically complete your tasks for you. This method circumvents most of the risk involved in automated computer tasking. That's because, in Import.io, every step depends upon human input. Consequently, these human-augmented interactions lower the risk that the machine will draw an incorrect conclusion because of overguessing.

Collecting images with ImageQuilts

ImageQuilts (www.imagequilts.com) is a Google Chrome extension developed in part by legendary Edward Tufte, one of the first great pioneers in data visualization — he popularized the metric "data-to-ink ratio" to judge the effectiveness of charts.

The task ImageQuilts performs is deceptively simple to describe but very complex to implement. ImageQuilts makes collages of tens of images, and pieces them all together into one "quilt" that's comprised of multiple rows of equal height. The reason this task is more complex than it may sound is that the source images are almost never the same height. ImageQuilts scrapes and resizes the images before stitching them together into one output image. The image quilt shown in Figure 17-1 was derived from a "Labeled for Reuse" Google Image Search of the term *data science*.

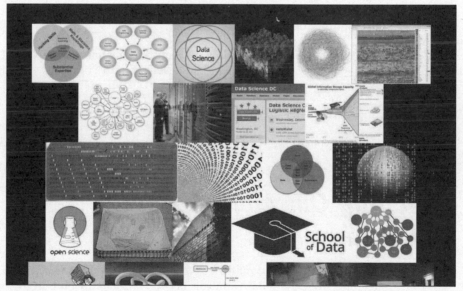

Figure 17-1: An ImageQuilts output from the Google Image search term *data science*.

ImageQuilts even allows you to choose the order of images or to randomize them. You can use the tool to drag and drop any image to any place, remove an image, zoom all images at once, or zoom each image individually. You can even use the tool to covert the images in color, grayscale, or *inverted color* — which is handy for making contact sheets of negatives, if you're one of those rare people who still processes analog photography.

Wrangling data with DataWrangler

DataWrangler (`http://vis.stanford.edu/wrangler`) is an online tool that's supported by the University of Washington Interactive Data Lab — but, at the time it was developed, this group was called the Stanford Visualization Group. This is the same group that developed Lyra (`www.idl.cs.washington.edu/projects/lyra`), an interactive data visualization environment that you can use to create complex visualizations without programming experience.

If your goal is to *sculpt* your dataset (or clean things up by moving things around like a sculptor would — split this part in two, slice off that bit and move it over there, push this down so that everything below it gets shifted to the right, and so on), DataWrangler is the tool for you.

The kinds of manipulations you can do with DataWrangler are similar to what you can do in Excel using Visual Basic. An example of this type of task is using DataWrangler or Excel with Visual Basic to copy, paste, and format information from lists on the Internet.

DataWrangler is so great that it suggests actions based on your dataset, and can even repeat complex actions across entire datasets — actions like eliminating skipped rows, splitting data from one column into two, turning a header into column data, and so on. DataWrangler is also great for showing you where there is missing data.

Missing data can indicate a formatting error that needs to be cleaned up.

Checking Out More Data Exploration Tools

Visualization is important for clarifying and communicating your data's meaning, but careful data analysis is even more important. In this section, I introduce you to a few free tools that you can use for some advanced data analysis tasks. These tools include Tableau Public, Gephi, and WEKA.

Talking about Tableau Public

Tableau Public (`http://public.tableausoftware.com`) is a free desktop application that aims to be a complete package for chart making. Tableau Public is just the free version of Tableau Desktop. As part of the freeware limitation, the application doesn't let you save files locally to your computer. All your work must be uploaded to Tableau Public's cloud server, unless you purchase the software.

Tableau Public creates three levels of document:

- ✔ **Worksheet:** The Worksheet is where you can create individual charts from data you've imported from Access, Excel, or a text-format CSV file. You can then use Tableau to easily do things like choose between different data graphic types or drag columns onto different axes or subgroups.

  There is a bit of a learning curve in getting to know the flow of the application and its nomenclature — for example, *dimensions* are categorical data while *measures* are numeric data.

  Tableau offers many different default chart types — bar charts, scatter plots, line charts, bubble charts, Gantt charts, and even geographical maps. Tableau Public can even look at the type of data you have and suggest types of charts that you can use to best represent it. As an example of this, imagine you have two dimensions and one measure. In this situation, a bar chart is a popular choice because you have two categories of data and only one numeric measure for those two categories. Whereas if you have two dimensions and two measures, a scatter plot may be a good option because the scatter plot data graphic allows you to visualize two sets of numerical data for two categories of data.

- ✔ **Dashboard:** You can use a Tableau Dashboard to combine charts with text annotations or with other data charts. You can also use the Dashboard to add interactive filters, like check boxes or sliders, so users can interact with your data to only visualize certain time series or categories.

- ✔ **Story:** With a Tableau Story, you can combine several dashboards in a sort of slideshow presentation that shows a linear story in your data.

You can use Tableau Public's online gallery to share all the worksheets, dashboards, and stories that you generate within the application. You can also embed them into websites that link back to the Tableau Public cloud server.

Getting up to speed in Gephi

Remember back in middle school how you were taught to use graph paper to do math and then draw graphs of the results? Well, apparently that nomenclature is incorrect. Those things with an *x*-axis and *y*-axis are actually called *charts*. *Graphs* are network topologies.

If this is your first introduction to network topologies, welcome to this weird and wonderful world. You're in for a voyage of discovery. Gephi (`https://gephi.org`) is an open-source software package you can use to create graph layouts and then manipulate them to get the most clear and effective results. The kinds of connection-based visualizations you can create in Gephi are very useful in *all types* of network analyses — from social media data analysis to an analysis of protein-protein interactions or horizontal gene transfers between bacteria.

To illustrate a network analysis, imagine that you want to analyze the interconnectedness of people in your social networks. Here, you can use Gephi to quickly and easily present the different aspects of interconnectedness between your Facebook friends. So, imagine that you're friends with Alice. You and Alice share 10 of the same friends on Facebook, but Alice also has an additional 200 friends with whom you are not connected. One of the friends you and Alice share is named Bob. You and Bob share 20 of the same friends on Facebook, too, but Bob has only 5 friends in common with Alice. On the basis of shared friends, it's easy to surmise that you and Bob are the most similar, but you can use Gephi to visually graph the friend links between yourself, Alice, and Bob.

Figure 17-2 is a moderate-sized graph that was created in the Gephi application. This graph shows which characters appear in the same chapter as which other characters in Victor Hugo's immense novel *Les Misérables*. The larger bubbles indicate that these characters appear most often, and the more lines attached to a bubble, the more he or she co-occurs with others — the big one in the center is Jean Valjean.

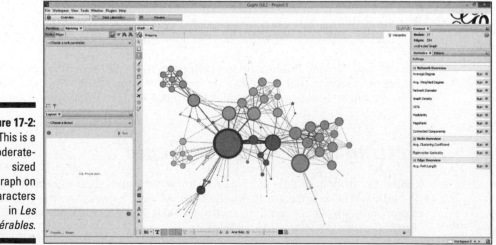

Figure 17-2: This is a moderate-sized graph on characters in *Les Misérables*.

When you use Gephi, the application automatically colors your data into different clusters. The cluster of characters in the upper-left of Figure 17-2 mostly only appear with each other (they're the friends of Fantine, like Félix Tholomyès — if you've only seen the musical, they don't appear in that production). These characters are only connected to the rest of the book's characters through one character, Fantine. Were there a group of characters that only appear together and never with any other characters, they would be in a separate cluster of their own and not attached to the rest of the graph in any way. This is how network analysis works and how it's done in the Gephi program.

Figure 17-3 shows a graph of the United States power grid, and the degrees of interconnectedness between thousands of power generation and power distribution facilities. This type of graph is commonly referred to as a *hairball graph,* for obvious reasons. There are ways to make it less dense and more visually clear, but doing this is as much of an art as it is a science.

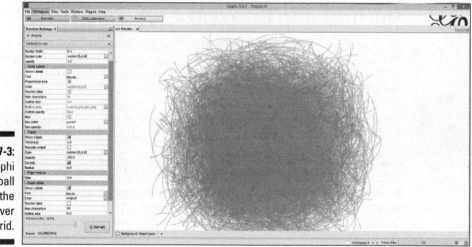

Figure 17-3: A Gephi hairball graph of the U.S. power grid.

Machine learning with the WEKA suite

Waikato Environment for Knowledge Analysis (WEKA; `www.cs.waikato.ac.nz/ml/weka`) is a popular suite of machine-learning tools that was written in Java and developed at the University of Waikato, New Zealand.

WEKA is a standalone application that you can use to analyze patterns in your datasets and then visualize those patterns in all sorts of interesting ways. For advanced users, WEKA's true value is derived from its suite of machine-learning algorithms that you can use to cluster or categorize your data. WEKA even allows you to run different machine-learning algorithms in parallel, to see which ones perform most efficiently. WEKA can be run through a graphical user interface (GUI) or by command line. Thanks to the very well-written "Weka Wiki" documentation, the learning curve for WEKA is not as steep as one would expect for a piece of software this powerful.

Checking Out More Web-Based Visualization Tools

You can use a variety of free web apps to easily generate unique and interesting data visualizations. The tools in this section are just two examples.

Getting a little Weave up your sleeve

Web-based Analysis and Visualization Environment, or Weave (www. oicweave.org), is the brainchild of Dr. Georges Grinstein at the University of Massachusetts, Lowell. Weave is an open-source, collaborative tool that uses Adobe Flash to display data visualizations.

Because Weave relies on Adobe Flash, it won't be accessible by all browsers, particularly those on Apple mobile devices — iPad, iPhone, and so on.

The Weave package is Java software designed to be run on a server with a database engine like MySQL or Oracle, although it can be run on a desktop computer so long as a local host server (like Apache Tomcat) and database software are both installed. Weave offers an excellent Wiki that explains all aspects of the program, including installation on Mac, Linux, or Windows.

Installing Weave on the Windows OS is easiest because of Weave's single installer that installs the desktop middleware, as well as the server, and database dependencies. For the installer to be able to install all this, though, you need to make sure that you've first installed the free Adobe Air run-time environment on your machine.

Weave is great because you can use it to automatically access countless open datasets or simply upload your own. You can use Weave to generate multiple interactive visualizations, like charts and maps that allow your users to efficiently explore even the most complex datasets.

If your goal is to create visualizations that allow your audience to see and explore the interrelatedness between subsets of your data, then Weave is the perfect tool for this type of task. Another awesome feature in Weave is that, if you update your underlying data source, your data visualizations update in real time also.

Figure 17-4 shows a demo visualization on Weave's own server. It depicts every county in the United States, with many columns of data from which to choose. In this example, the map shows county-level obesity data on employed women who are 16 years of age and older. The chart at the bottom left shows that there's a correlation between obesity and unemployment in this group.

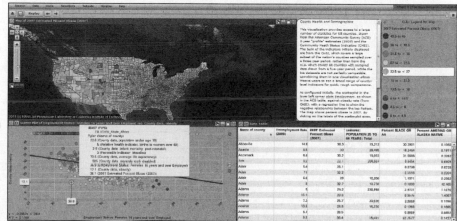

Figure 17-4:
A chart, map, and data table in Weave.

Checking out Knoema's data visualization offerings

You can use Knoema's (www.knoema.com) data-visualization tools to create visualizations that enable your audience to easily explore data, drill down on geographic areas or on different indicators, and automatically produce data-driven timelines. Using Knoema, you can quickly export all results into PowerPoint files, Excel files, PDFs, JPG images, or PNG images, or even embed them on your website.

If you embed the data visualizations in a webpage of your website, those visualizations will automatically update if you make changes to the underlying dataset.

Figure 17-5 shows a chart and a table that were automatically generated with just two mouse clicks in Knoema. One click was to select indicators by country, and the other was to select Urban Population (percent of total). From here, the data can be exported, further explored, saved, or embedded in an external website.

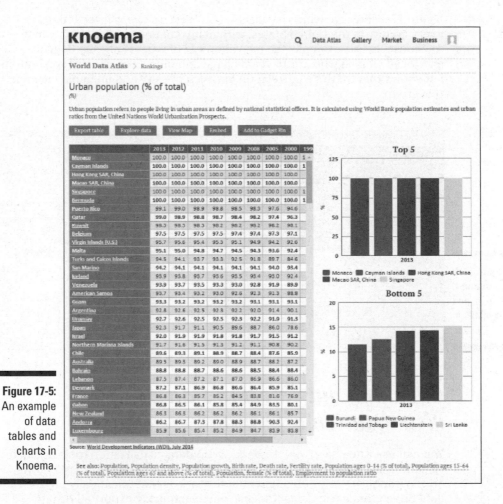

Figure 17-5:
An example
of data
tables and
charts in
Knoema.

You can use Knoema to make your own dashboards, too. You can make dashboards from your own data or from open data in Knoema's repository. Figures 17-6 and 17-7 show dashboards that were quickly created from Knoema's Eurostat data on capital and financial accounts.

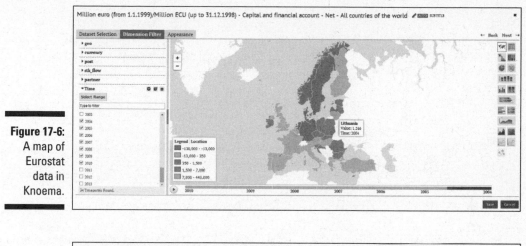

Figure 17-6:
A map of
Eurostat
data in
Knoema.

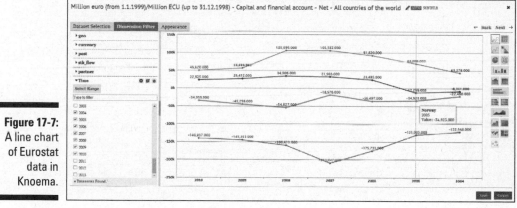

Figure 17-7:
A line chart
of Eurostat
data in
Knoema.

Part VI
Appendixes

In this part . . .

- ✔ Find resources for more information on big data.
- ✔ Look up key terms in a glossary.

Appendix A

Resources

• •

*S*taying current on tools and trends is always a challenge in emerging technologies. There's good news though. An abundance of resources, vendor research, webcasts, and *standards groups* (groups that promote best practices) await you online, where you can learn new tools and keep up on the latest vendor news and offerings.

Vendor Websites

With more than 1,000 companies that have big data products or services, I can't list them all. Instead, the following list includes the major players in the big data space:

✔ **Amazon Web Services (http://aws.amazon.com/big-data):** Amazon Web Services offers a set of cloud services around big data storage and computing resources.

✔ **Big Data University (www.bigdatauniversity.com):** Big Data University is an online community dedicated to educating people on big data. It's funded by IBM and is free.

✔ **Birst (www.birst.com):** Birst is a cloud-based business intelligence and analytics tool.

✔ **Cloudera (www.cloudera.com):** Cloudera provides software, training, and support for the Apache Hadoop framework.

✔ **Couchbase (http://couchbase.com):** Couchbase is a NoSQL document database for interactive web applications.

✔ **EMC (http://bigdatablog.emc.com):** EMC is a hardware vendor providing storage for on-site big data analytics processing.

✔ **Google (http://research.google.com):** Google has a host of tools and services that helps developers deliver big data solutions. BigQuery is one of those products, focused solely on big data. It also offers visualization tools and cloud computing services (see Chapter 7).

✔ **Hortonworks (http://hortonworks.com):** Hortonworks is a framework for using open-source Hadoop in the enterprise.

- ✔ **IBM Netezza** (`www.netezza.com`): Netezza is an on-site data warehouse appliance.

- ✔ **Informatica** (`www.informatica.com/bigdata`): Informatica provides tools for data integration and migration. Its big data offerings help couple traditional databases and NoSQL data stores to make data integration easy for big data processing.

- ✔ **Jaspersoft** (`http://jaspersoft.com`): Jaspersoft provides open-source analytics tools for data visualization from the dashboard.

- ✔ **MapR** (`http://mapr.com`): MapR is a complete distribution system for Apache Hadoop.

- ✔ **Microsoft** (`www.microsoft.com/enterprise/it-trends/big-data`): Microsoft uses its Azure cloud platform and Azure HDInsight products for analytics.

- ✔ **MicroStrategy** (`www.microstrategy.com`): MicroStrategy delivers business intelligence and analytics tools to large and medium-size businesses.

- ✔ **MongoDB** (`www.mongodb.com`): This is an open-source document-centric NoSQL database. It's the most popular NoSQL database today.

- ✔ **Oracle** (`www.oracle.com/us/technologies/big-data`): Oracle is the creator of the world's most widely used relational database management system (RDMS). It also creates in-memory database systems and manages the open-source MySQL Database Management System.

- ✔ **Pentaho** (`www.pentaho.com`): This is an open-source business analytics tool.

- ✔ **Predictive Analytics Today** (`www.predictiveanalyticstoday.com/top-30-software-for-text-analysis-text-mining-text-analytics`): This is a curated software list for text analytics.

- ✔ **Qlik** (`www.qlik.com`): Qlik is business intelligence and visualization software.

- ✔ **RapidMiner** (`www.rapidminder.com`): RapidMiner is an open-source analytics modeling software application. It's used for statistical analysis.

- ✔ **SAP** (`www.sap.com/solution/big-data`): SAP is one of the world's largest enterprise software firms. It provides business intelligence tools, cloud services, SAP HANA, and in-memory database systems for big data analytics.

- ✔ **SAS** (`www.sas.com/en_us/insights/big-data.html`): The world's largest privately held software company, SAS provides the premier statistical analytics software package.

- ✔ **Splunk** (`www.splunk.com`): Splunk is a big data analytics tool used for the analysis and collection of machine data.

- **Spotfire (`http://spotfire.tibco.com`):** Spotfire, now owned by Tibco, provides business intelligence and visualization tools.

- **Sumo Logic (`www.sumologic.com`):** Sumo Logic is a cloud-based analytics engine that specializes in log file analysis.

- **Tableau Software (`www.tableausoftware.com`):** Tableau produces dynamic and interactive visualization software for big data and analytics.

- **Teradata (`http://bigdata.teradata.com`):** Teradata builds high-end data warehouse software for high-performance analytics systems.

Bookmark the VentureBeat article on the big data ecosystem at `www.venturebeat.com/2014/05/11/the-state-of-big-data-in-2014-chart`. This article has a chart of the current big data ecosystem version 3.0 (which is three versions ahead of its famous 1.0 list of ecosystem companies published a few years ago). In technology, an *ecosystem* is a collection of a company's products and services in a given industry (in this case, big data).

Standards Organizations

As technologies gain traction within organizations, people tend to organize groups to drive standards and best practices. Several active groups working today foster standards around security, exchanges, and best practices:

- **The Cloud Security Alliance Big Data Working Group (BDWG; `https://cloudsecurityalliance.org/research/big-data`):** The BDWG is a subset group within the Cloud Security Alliance whose purpose is to find scalable and secure solutions to use big data in the cloud.

- **The National Institute of Standards and Technology (`www.nist.gov`):** NIST is a federal technology agency that has been part of the U.S. federal government since 1901. Its goal is to build standards for measurement to propel U.S. firms in a leadership position globally. For big data, the focus of the NIST is to enable research and discovery of best practices to push.

- **OASIS group (`www.oasis-open.org/committees/tc_cat.php?cat=bigdata`):** This group promotes open standards in the information industry.

- **The Object Management Group (OMG; `www.omg.org`):** The OMG is a consortium of member firms that collaborate to solidify standards across multiple technology sectors.

- **The Open Data Foundation (`www.opendatafoundation.org`):** The Open Data Foundation is a nonprofit working on a global scale to drive *metadata* standards for the use of statistical data across every industry.

Metadata is information about data; it describes data to ensure compatibility between systems and fosters standards among companies and industries.

✔ **The Open Group** (`http://blog.opengroup.org/tag/big-data`): The Open Group works with customers and vendors to build standards and interoperability.

Open-Source Projects

The Apache Software Foundation is a nonprofit group that administers the community development of key technologies within big data. Because Apache solutions are delivered under the Apache License, users and organizations can utilize, change, and distribute the software without having to pay royalties. Many very important big data projects are vetted by the Apache Foundation.

The following is a list of important Apache Foundation Projects related to big data:

✔ **Accumulo** (`http://accumulo.apache.org`): A secure implementation of Google's BigTable.

✔ **Cassandra** (`http://cassandra.apache.org`): A distributed database system originally developed by Facebook with a focus on fast access.

✔ **CouchDB** (`http://couchdb.apache.org`): A NoSQL document-oriented database.

✔ **Flume** (`http://flume.apache.org`): This is a distributed system to collect, aggregate, and transport large amounts of log data generated from web site traffic.

✔ **Hadoop** (`http://hadoop.apache.org`): Large-scale processing of distributed datasets, including the following:

  • **Hadoop Common:** The collection of software libraries used by other modules

  • **Hadoop Distributed Files System (HDFS):** The core file system that stores data across computers providing huge power when aggregated

  • **Hadoop YARN:** A resource manager for scheduling and streamlining MapReduce jobs

  • **Hadoop MapReduce:** A model for processing large datasets

✔ **HBase** (`http://hbase.apache.org`): Manages real-time read/write access to big data files.

✔ **Mahout** (`http://mahout.apache.org`): An open-source machine-learning framework.

✔ **MongoDB (www.mongodb.org):** A document-oriented database system that is *cross-platform* (able to run on many operating systems).

✔ **Python (www.python.org):** A powerful scripting programming language.

✔ **Solr (http://lucene.apache.org/solr):** Supports full text search for text analytics.

✔ **Spark (http://spark.apache.org):** An Apache project built upon the Hadoop Distributed Files System (HDFS); can deliver up to 100 times the speed that traditional MapReduce systems, like Hadoop, can.

✔ **Sqoop (http://sqoop.apache.org):** Aallows for relational data to be moved into a Hadoop data store.

✔ **ZooKeeper (http://zookeeper.apache.org):** A framework to create and manage redundant software systems.

Big Data Conferences and Trade Shows

Conferences and trade shows are an excellent way to stay connected to the community, get hands-on experience in boot camps and labs, and hear from the leaders in the industry. New conferences are added every year, but here are a few important ones to attend:

✔ **AWS ReInvent:** Amazon Web Services' annual user event in Las Vegas. This popular event has thousands of cloud and big data professionals and AWS partners, and covers the latest in AWS technology.

✔ **Big Data TechCon:** Big Data TechCon is big data conference with hands-on training, seminars, and an expo of the latest in big data technology. It's usually held in the fall in San Francisco.

✔ **The Data Warehouse Institute (TDWI):** The TDWI hosts many events throughout the year. It's supported widely by key vendors in the industry.

✔ **IEEE International Congress on Big Data:** Provides an international forum to explore big data topics.

✔ **Gigaom Structure Data:** A conference on big data's impact on the information economy.

✔ **Hadoop World:** Collocated with Strata, Hadoop World is the biggest conference for Hadoop users and is sponsored by leading Hadoop vendors.

✔ **O'Reilly Strata Conference:** An extremely popular series that hosts multiple events around the world promoting big data, education, and research.

Strata has a great Twitter feed (http://twitter.com/strataconf), which is kept current with information about technologies, speakers, and trends.

Leading Analysts Research Group

A huge amount of resources are spent on research to help businesses make informed decisions about technology. All these research groups are major influencers in the world of technology and big data. Take time to familiarize yourself with their reports and analysis. You can use this information to spot trends in the market, select the best technology for your needs, and stay current with leading-edge thinking. The term *thought leader* has lost much of its value today, but these firms are among those that still can retain their claim on the term:

- **Aberdeen Group** (`www.aberdeen.com`)**:** This group provides custom business intelligence research to help companies improve their overall performance.

- **The Data Warehouse Institute** (`www.tdwi.org`)**:** A nonprofit organization that has provided training, certification, conferences, and research for all things data since 1995.

- **Forrester Research** (`www.forrester.com`)**:** Forrester Research is a technology market research firm. It publishes *Forrester Playbooks* to guide firms through technology adoption. You can find a list of publications at `https://www.forrester.com/marketing/playbooks-all.html`. The Forrester Wave is a tool to evaluate technology vendors.

- **Gartner** (`www.gartner.com`)**:** Gartner is a leading technology research and analysis firm, famous for its technology hype cycles and Magic Quadrant research methodology. The hype cycles have been used for years to help professionals understand the maturity of technology by mapping the development on an adoption curve. The Magic Quadrant maps vendors in a matrix measuring maturity of technology vendors.

- **International Data Corporation** (IDC; `www.idc.com`)**:** IDC is an independent research firm covering many global market segments, including big data.

- **McKinsey Global Institute** (`www.mckinsey.com/insights/mgi`)**:** The McKinsey Global Institute is part of McKinsey & Company, one of the world's most trusted advisory firms. Its influence reaches across private, public, and social sectors. The 2011 McKinsey Report on big data was a seminal piece of published research, coinciding with a tidal wave of interest in big data globally.

Appendix B

Glossary

· ·

aggregating: Summarizing a collection of data.

agile: A framework for developing software or a product that focuses on small iteration cycles (usually two to four weeks), heavy stakeholder interaction, and delivery of functional product at each cycle.

AI: *See* artificial intelligence.

algorithm: A mathematical formula used to analyze data.

analytics: A field of study around data; the results of data analysis.

anonymization: The process of removing personally identifiable data about a person.

application: Computer software written to perform some function.

artificial intelligence (AI): A field of study with the goal of allowing machines to process in a similar way to humans. Allows for computer systems to "learn" and improve with more information.

behavioral analytics: Analytics that look at how humans act with the goal to predict future actions. Human pattern analysis.

big data scientist: Someone who develops the algorithms to make sense out of big data.

big data startup: A young company that has developed new big data technology.

bioinformatics: The analytical field of study pertaining to life science and medicine.

biometrics: The identification of humans by their characteristics like facial features, fingerprints, and other distinguishing marks.

business intelligence: Attempts to look at historical data to better understand business trends.

cloud computing: A distributed computing system used for data storage and computing power that is not located on the user's premises. There are several key attributes of cloud computing that make it different from a traditional system:

- *Elasticity:* The system grows or shrinks automatically with the demands of the user.
- *Geography:* Users can push their applications to various geographic regions.
- *No capital expense:* Users do not need to purchase the systems outright. They pay for what they use, like a utility.

comparative analysis: Process of data comparisons and calculations to detect patterns within very large datasets.

concurrency: Performing multiple similar tasks at the same time.

correlation analysis: A method of determining relationships among data or events.

CRM: *See* customer relationship management.

customer relationship management (CRM): A system for managing sales, sales forecasts, and customers.

cybersecurity: The act of protecting technology, information, and networks from attacks.

dashboard: A visual representation of data.

data aggregation tools: Tools for bringing disparate data together for analysis.

data analyst: Someone who analyzes, models, cleans, or processes data.

data center: A physical location that houses the servers for storing data.

data cleansing: The process of reviewing and revising data in order to delete duplicates, correct errors, and provide consistency.

data custodian: Someone who is responsible for the technical environment necessary for data storage.

data ethical guidelines: Guidelines that help organizations be transparent with their data, ensuring simplicity, security, and privacy.

data feed: A stream of data, such as a Twitter feed or RSS. *See also* RSS.

data marketplace: An online environment for buying and selling datasets.

data mart: Related to a data warehouse, but usually smaller and more focused on one subject area. *See also* data warehouse.

data mining: The process of finding data patterns from datasets.

data modeling: The process of architecting data objects and structures as they relate to a business or other context.

data virtualization: A data integration process used to gain more insights. Usually it involves databases, applications, file systems, websites, big data techniques, and so on.

data warehouse: A data store used for decision support. Data warehouses are not often real time and are organized in a way to make data analysis easy. Unlike data marts, data warehouses contain multiple subject areas.

database: A collection of data stored digitally.

database as a service (DBaaS): A database hosted in the cloud on a pay-per-use basis (for example, Amazon Relational Database Service or Oracle Database as Service).

database management system: A system for collecting, storing, and providing access to data.

dataset: A collection of data.

DBaaS: *See* database as a service.

deidentification: *See* anonymization.

discriminant analysis: A statistical method for predicting a grouping of data.

distributed file system: A system that offers simplified, highly available access to storing, analyzing, and processing data.

document store database: A document-oriented database used to store, manage, and retrieve documents objects. Also known as *semi-structured data*.

ETL: *See* extract, transform, and load.

exabyte: 1,000 petabytes or 1 billion gigabytes.

extract, transform, and load (ETL): A process in databases and data warehousing that involves extracting the data from different sources, transforming it to fit specific needs, and loading it into a logical database.

failover: Switching automatically to one system if another fails.

fault-tolerant design: A system designed to work in the event of a disruption.

geospatial data: Data that defines geographic information.

graph database: A database that uses graph structures with edges, properties, and nodes.

grid computing: Connecting many computer system locations, often via the cloud, working together for the same purpose.

Hadoop: An open-source framework that is built to process and store huge amounts of data across a distributed file system.

Hadoop Distributed File System (HDFS): A distributed file system designed to run on commodity hardware. *See also* distributed file system.

HBase: An open-source, nonrelational, distributed database running in conjunction with Hadoop. *See also* Hadoop.

HDFS: *See* Hadoop Distributed File System.

high-performance computing (HPC): Using supercomputers or huge clusters to solve highly complex computing problems.

HPC: *See* high-performance computing.

in memory: When a database management system stores data on the main memory instead of the disk, resulting is very fast processing, storing, and loading of the data.

Internet of things: Ordinary devices that are connected to the Internet at any time, anywhere, via sensors.

key-value database: A simple database that stores data with a primary key.

latency: A measure of time delayed in a system.

legacy system: An old system or technology.

load balancing: The process of distributing workloads or network traffic across multiple servers.

log file: A file automatically created by a computer to record events that occur while the system is running.

M2M data: *See* machine-to-machine data.

machine data: Data automatically created by systems via sensors or algorithms.

machine learning: A subset of AI, in which machines learn from what they're doing and become better over time. *See also* artificial intelligence.

machine-to-machine (M2M) data: Data used by machines or clusters of machines that are communicating with each other.

MapReduce: A software framework for processing vast amounts of data.

mash up: Bringing together different information to communicate a single idea.

massively parallel processing (MPP): Using many different processors to perform tasks at the same time.

megabyte: Approximately 1,000 bytes.

metadata: Data about data. Metadata gives information about what the data is about.

MongoDB: An open-source NoSQL database.

MPP: *See* massively parallel processing.

multidimensional database: A database used to process online analytical processing (OLAP) applications and often the framework for data warehousing.

MultiValue database: A type of NoSQL and multidimensional database that understands three-dimensional data directly.

natural language processing (NLP): An area of computer science involved with the computational study of human languages.

network analysis: Analyzing connections between computers in a network. Looks at connectivity, speed, and latency.

NLP: *See* natural language processing.

NoSQL: A database that doesn't adhere to relational database structures. Used to organize and query unstructured data.

Not Only SQL: *See* NoSQL.

object database: A database that stores data in the form of objects. Object databases are different from relational structures and can be used to store unstructured or semi-structured data.

OLAP: *See* online analytical processing.

OLTP: *See* online transaction processing.

online analytical processing (OLAP): Systems that are multidimensional data stores used to perform analysis on large datasets. Usually used for business intelligence systems.

online transaction processing (OLTP): Systems that manage transactional data, like banking or ATM systems.

ontology: The study of how things relate. Used in big data to analyze seemingly unrelated data to discover insights.

operational database: A database system that runs core functions to the business in production environments. These are not test or reporting database systems, but actual systems that run the operations of the company.

optimization analysis: The process of using algorithms to improve performance of a system or analysis.

orthogonal: In statistics, data that are independent of each other. In big data, we seek to understand if orthogonal information is, in fact, related.

outlier: An object or data point that deviates significantly from the general average.

outlier detection: A set of algorithms to automatically discover outliers within a dataset.

PaaS: *See* platform as a service.

pattern recognition: The process of identifying patterns in data via algorithms to make predictions within a subject area.

petabyte: Approximately 1,000 terabytes or 1 million gigabytes.

Pig: A programming interface for programmers to create MapReduce jobs within Hadoop.

platform as a service (PaaS): A service providing all the necessary infrastructure for cloud-computing solutions.

predictive analysis: Analysis that is used to predict behavior or events. This can be from historical data, social data, or any other orthogonal datasets. *See also* orthogonal.

primary key: A uniquely identifiable record used for fast data lookup.

privacy: The ability of a person to keep personal information to himself or herself.

public data: Public information or datasets that were created for general use, with public and private funding.

query: A question; in the context of data, it's often a set of code used to ask a question of a dataset.

real-time data: Data that is created while a process or event is happening.

real-time streaming: The process of capturing, storing, and analyzing real-time data. *See also* real-time data.

recommendation engine: An algorithm that suggests actions based on past behavior of the user or similar users.

regression analysis: Analysis used to discover the dependency between variables.

relational online analytical processing (ROLAP): The process of automatically creating analysis and the coinciding tables to research relational data stores.

ROLAP: *See* relational online analytical processing.

routing analysis: Analysis using many different variables to find the optimized routing for a certain means of transport in order to decrease fuel costs and increase efficiency.

RSS: A standard by which Internet feeds can publish news or other information to subscribers. Stands for *Really Simple Syndication.*

SaaS: *See* software as a service.

Semi-structured data: A structured data type that does not have a formal definition, like a document. It has tags or other markers to enforce a hierarchy of records within a particular object, but may be different from another object. *See also* structured data.

sentiment analysis: Analysis to find out how people feel based on digital communication like Twitter, Instagram, or emails.

signal analysis: Analysis that looks at information over a given amount of time. It can be sound, data stream, or even image feeds. It is often used with sensor data.

simulation: The imitation of a real-world event in order to predict behavior or analyze patterns.

smart grid: Sensors within an energy grid used to monitor what is going on in real time, helping to increase efficiency.

social media: User-curated systems where groups of people are networked together to collaborate or share information.

software as a service (SaaS): A software tool available via web clients and usually paid for through a subscription-type model.

SQL: A programming language for retrieving data from a relational database.

structured data: Data that adheres to a strict definition.

terabyte: Approximately 1,000 gigabytes.

time series analysis: The analysis of data obtained through a recurring measurement of time.

transactional data: Information stored from a time-based instance, like a bank deposit or phone call.

unstructured data: Data that doesn't fit into a fixed and strict definition. Things like sound files, images, text, and web pages can be considered unstructured data.

value: The benefit for stakeholders derived from bringing together massive amounts of information.

variability: The ever-changing nature of data. For example, you may want to store tweets, bank records, and weather.

variety: The difference in type of data. Data today comes in many different formats: unstructured data, semi-structured data, structured data, and even complex structured data.

velocity: The speed at which data is created, stored, analyzed, and reported.

visualization: The process of bringing very complex analysis into a visual representation that users can understand.

volume: The massive amounts of data to be stored and analyzed.

weather data: Public datasets that can be used by organizations wanting to combine weather information with other data sources.

yottabyte: Approximately 1,000 zettabytes, equivalent to about 250 trillion DVDs.

zettabyte: Approximately 1,000 exabytes or 1 billion terabytes.

Index

● S ●

About the Author

Jason Williamson is an assistant professor at the University of Virginia's McIntire School of Commerce. His interests include project management, cloud computing, data integration, and analysis. He also served his country in the United States Marine Corps. He holds an MS in Management of IT from the University of Virginia and a BS in Information Systems from Virginia Commonwealth University. His favorite job is husband to his wife and father to four children.

Jason has worked with the world's leading Fortune 1000 firms, including Oracle, General Electric, and Capital One. In addition to working in the corporate world, Jason was the founder and CTO for the construction industry's first SaaS/CRM offering. He led BuildLinks from a concept to a multi-million-dollar company and forged key financial and business partnerships with Sprint/Nextel and Intuit, helping to create innovative products. His creative thinking and vision opened the door for him to establish a nonprofit NGO dedicated to entrepreneurial and technology education in developing nations, which enabled the establishment of multiple self-sustaining companies in Latin America.

Dedication

I want to dedicate this work to my loving wife, Susan. She is truly a modern Proverbs 31 woman. Her leadership, faithfulness, hard work, and love are examples for me and all who know her.

Author's Acknowledgments

Thanks to all the amazing people at Wiley who worked with me to get this done — Andy Cummings, Amy Fandrei, Mark Enochs, and Connie Santisteban. Thanks to my agent, Matt Wagner, for opening the doors and making things happen. Thanks to Amit Okhandiar, president of mLogica, for providing research and content for some of the case studies. Also, thanks to Daniel Johnson and Sean Curry for some collaboration during our days at Virginia.

Publisher's Acknowledgments

Acquisitions Editor: Amy Fandrei

Project Editor: Elizabeth Kuball

Copy Editor: Elizabeth Kuball

Technical Editor: Tom Laszewski

Editorial Assistant: Claire Johnson

Sr. Editorial Assistant: Cherie Case

Project Coordinator: Sheree Montgomery

Contributors: Mike Wessler, Stephanie Diamond, Lillian Pierson

Cover Image: © iStock.com/Oko_SwanOmurphy

Apple & Mac

iPad For Dummies,
6th Edition
978-1-118-72306-7

iPhone For Dummies,
7th Edition
978-1-118-69083-3

Macs All-in-One
For Dummies, 4th Edition
978-1-118-82210-4

OS X Mavericks
For Dummies
978-1-118-69188-5

Blogging & Social Media

Facebook For Dummies,
5th Edition
978-1-118-63312-0

Social Media Engagement
For Dummies
978-1-118-53019-1

WordPress For Dummies,
6th Edition
978-1-118-79161-5

Business

Stock Investing
For Dummies, 4th Edition
978-1-118-37678-2

Investing For Dummies,
6th Edition
978-0-470-90545-6

Personal Finance
For Dummies, 7th Edition
978-1-118-11785-9

QuickBooks 2014
For Dummies
978-1-118-72005-9

Small Business Marketing
Kit For Dummies,
3rd Edition
978-1-118-31183-7

Careers

Job Interviews
For Dummies, 4th Edition
978-1-118-11290-8

Job Searching with Social
Media For Dummies,
2nd Edition
978-1-118-67856-5

Personal Branding
For Dummies
978-1-118-11792-7

Resumes For Dummies,
6th Edition
978-0-470-87361-8

Starting an Etsy Business
For Dummies, 2nd Edition
978-1-118-59024-9

Diet & Nutrition

Belly Fat Diet For Dummies
978-1-118-34585-6

Mediterranean Diet
For Dummies
978-1-118-71525-3

Nutrition For Dummies,
5th Edition
978-0-470-93231-5

Digital Photography

Digital SLR Photography
All-in-One For Dummies,
2nd Edition
978-1-118-59082-9

Digital SLR Video &
Filmmaking For Dummies
978-1-118-36598-4

Photoshop Elements 12
For Dummies
978-1-118-72714-0

Gardening

Herb Gardening
For Dummies, 2nd Edition
978-0-470-61778-6

Gardening with Free-Range
Chickens For Dummies
978-1-118-54754-0

Health

Boosting Your Immunity
For Dummies
978-1-118-40200-9

Diabetes For Dummies,
4th Edition
978-1-118-29447-5

Living Paleo For Dummies
978-1-118-29405-5

Big Data

Big Data For Dummies
978-1-118-50422-2

Data Visualization
For Dummies
978-1-118-50289-1

Hadoop For Dummies
978-1-118-60755-8

Language &
Foreign Language

500 Spanish Verbs
For Dummies
978-1-118-02382-2

English Grammar
For Dummies, 2nd Edition
978-0-470-54664-2

French All-in-One
For Dummies
978-1-118-22815-9

German Essentials
For Dummies
978-1-118-18422-6

Italian For Dummies,
2nd Edition
978-1-118-00465-4

e Available in print and e-book formats.

Available wherever books are sold. **For more information or to order direct visit www.dummies.com**

Math & Science

Algebra I For Dummies,
2nd Edition
978-0-470-55964-2

Anatomy and Physiology
For Dummies, 2nd Edition
978-0-470-92326-9

Astronomy For Dummies,
3rd Edition
978-1-118-37697-3

Biology For Dummies,
2nd Edition
978-0-470-59875-7

Chemistry For Dummies,
2nd Edition
978-1-118-00730-3

1001 Algebra II Practice
Problems For Dummies
978-1-118-44662-1

Microsoft Office

Excel 2013 For Dummies
978-1-118-51012-4

Office 2013 All-in-One
For Dummies
978-1-118-51636-2

PowerPoint 2013
For Dummies
978-1-118-50253-2

Word 2013 For Dummies
978-1-118-49123-2

Music

Blues Harmonica
For Dummies
978-1-118-25269-7

Guitar For Dummies,
3rd Edition
978-1-118-11554-1

iPod & iTunes
For Dummies, 10th Edition
978-1-118-50864-0

Programming

Beginning Programming
with C For Dummies
978-1-118-73763-7

Excel VBA Programming
For Dummies, 3rd Edition
978-1-118-49037-2

Java For Dummies,
6th Edition
978-1-118-40780-6

Religion & Inspiration

The Bible For Dummies
978-0-7645-5296-0

Buddhism For Dummies,
2nd Edition
978-1-118-02379-2

Catholicism For Dummies,
2nd Edition
978-1-118-07778-8

Self-Help & Relationships

Beating Sugar Addiction
For Dummies
978-1-118-54645-1

Meditation For Dummies,
3rd Edition
978-1-118-29144-3

Seniors

Laptops For Seniors
For Dummies, 3rd Edition
978-1-118-71105-7

Computers For Seniors
For Dummies, 3rd Edition
978-1-118-11553-4

iPad For Seniors
For Dummies, 6th Edition
978-1-118-72826-0

Social Security
For Dummies
978-1-118-20573-0

Smartphones & Tablets

Android Phones
For Dummies, 2nd Edition
978-1-118-72030-1

Nexus Tablets
For Dummies
978-1-118-77243-0

Samsung Galaxy S 4
For Dummies
978-1-118-64222-1

Samsung Galaxy Tabs
For Dummies
978-1-118-77294-2

Test Prep

ACT For Dummies,
5th Edition
978-1-118-01259-8

ASVAB For Dummies,
3rd Edition
978-0-470-63760-9

GRE For Dummies,
7th Edition
978-0-470-88921-3

Officer Candidate Tests
For Dummies
978-0-470-59876-4

Physician's Assistant Exam
For Dummies
978-1-118-11556-5

Series 7 Exam For Dummies
978-0-470-09932-2

Windows 8

Windows 8.1 All-in-One
For Dummies
978-1-118-82087-2

Windows 8.1 For Dummies
978-1-118-82121-3

Windows 8.1 For Dummies,
Book + DVD Bundle
978-1-118-82107-7

e Available in print and e-book formats.

Available wherever books are sold. **For more information or to order direct visit www.dummies.com**

Leverage the Power

For Dummies is the global leader in the reference category and one of the most trusted and highly regarded brands in the world. No longer just focused on books, customers now have access to the For Dummies content they need in the format they want. Let us help you develop a solution that will fit your brand and help you connect with your customers.

Advertising & Sponsorships

Connect with an engaged audience on a powerful multimedia site, and position your message alongside expert how-to content.

Targeted ads • Video • Email marketing • Microsites • Sweepstakes sponsorship

21 Million Monthly Page Views & 13 Million Unique Visitors

# of For Dummies

Custom Publishing

Reach a global audience in any language by creating a solution that will differentiate you from competitors, amplify your message, and encourage customers to make a buying decision.

Apps • Books • eBooks • Video • Audio • Webinars

Brand Licensing & Content

Leverage the strength of the world's most popular reference brand to reach new audiences and channels of distribution.

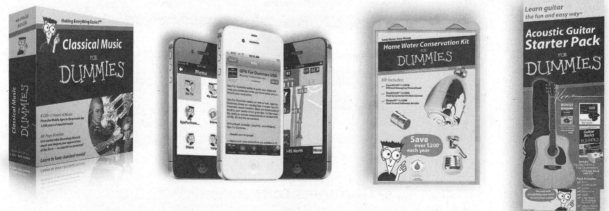

For more information, visit www.Dummies.com/biz

FOR DUMMIES
A Wiley Brand

Dummies products make life easier!

- DIY
- Consumer Electronics
- Crafts
- Software
- Cookware
- Hobbies
- Videos
- Music
- Games
- and More!

For more information, go to **Dummies.com** and search the store by category.

FOR
DUMMIES
A Wiley Brand